The Book of Inner Strength

Ian Muir

14 Croydon Road, Waddon,
Croydon, Surrey CR0 4PA
+44 (0)208 688 2598
Fax +44 (0)870 116 3530
info@filamentpublishing.com

Printed by IngramSpark
Design layout Charlotte Mouncey
Cover Photographs Ian Muir

ISBN 978-1-905493-14-2

This Book is dedicated to my wife Ingrid and the many people I have met and worked with; the experiences they have given me; the lessons I have learned and so many things I have been lucky to observe.

It is also dedicated to the people of Menorca, who over centuries have endured waves of conquests and reconquests. And yet they remain predominantly proud, confident and strong.

The front cover photograph is of a Taula south of Maó, Menorca's capital. This stone structure is more than two thousand years old. Amid the rubble stands a pillar of strength, supporting an impossible weight. There are many of these structures across the island. For me, they symbolise the essence of inner strength: cool, calm, confident, supportive, visible and serene among the chaos.

The back cover shows the San Roc medieval gateway tower in Maó. Having stood for centuries, for me it epitomises towering resilience.

Edward Lee Isler is the managing partner at Isler Dare Ray and Radcliffe, PC, a law firm, based at Tyson's Corner, Washington, Virginia, USA. His clients can face stressful legal matters. Eddie wrote: "Many published books, while momentarily entertaining, are destined to end up forgotten on our bookshelves. Mr. Muir has created a piece of work that will serve as a continuing inspiration and encouragement for those seeking to navigate many of life's challenges and pitfalls."

Mark Withers is a business and organisational transformation consultant in the United Kingdom. He works with organisations to improve their performance and confront difficult issues. He wrote: "This book makes you smile and it makes you think. It scans the complexities of modern living and brings into focus the things that really matter."

Stuart Lindenfield, an international authority on business networking, author and senior manager of Reed Consulting, is based in both the United Kingdom and Spain. Having read this book, he commented: "A real treasure trove of paradigm-shifting spirit-lifting aphorisms. Great for dipping into when the creative juices need a boost."

Gisela Klinkhammer is a German senior public sector lawyer dealing with complex cross-border issues. Based near Cologne, she travels extensively in Europe and wrote: "This light hearted look at life is easy to follow but it contains immensely powerful advice."

Taro Ogawa is a human resources manager working for

ADC Asia Pacific Abbott. He is based in Tokyo, Japan and after due consideration wrote: "Congratulations on finalizing such a valuable book in your life. It took me a while to get back to you because I wanted more time to read it completely since I would like to understand your real message in the book. This book has relevance to many different cultures and speaks to both East and West."

Diane Smith works in Customer Operations for British Airways at London Heathrow Airport, United Kingdom. Having read The Book of Inner Strength, she said: "We all know how busy and stressful the world's major airports can get. This helpful guide enables people to step back and take stock before facing the next challenge, renewed and refreshed. I can think of quite a few people who will get lasting pleasure from The Book of Inner Strength."

Michael Winslow is a non executive director and business performance coach. Based in the United Kingdom, he works in both the UK and Europe helping senior business leaders achieve their goals. Michael said: "This book of inner strength will be extremely valuable to anyone who wants to significantly raise their game and improve their performance both personally and professionally. It will also be a useful resource to assist and support the individual during times of difficulty."

Fiona Colquhoun is a Director at CEDR – the Centre for Effective Disputes Resolution. This highly respected and internationally renowned organisation specialises in mediation as an alternative to formal disputes. Almost all their successes are confidential, however their work resolves complex commercial problems, sometimes involving tens of millions of pounds. Fiona wrote: "The reader will find his or her story in each quotation." She also added that a pessimist sees the difficulty in every opportunity whereas an optimist sees the opportunity in every difficulty.

Mark Perks is both a vineyard owner and viticulturalist in Tasmania, Australia. Mark commented "Despite the philosophical title, this book has practical value, and not just for burnt out business people!"

Praise for The Book of Inner Strength
Second edition

Rilson Santos, is a senior manager within an Industrial Engineering Group, based in Belo Horizonte, Brazil. He commented: "This is a great help to reduce pressure and enable people to focus on achieving their goals."

Li Min Lim is a regional Head of HR for South East Asia, based in Singapore. She said: "You seemed to predict the global events of 2008 onwards by helping people prepare for them. My team has drawn very valuable lessons and inspiration from your writing. You help us perform better by understanding ourselves and others around us much better."

Nazmi Adams is a board member of a professional institute and a Global Head of Marketing. Based in South Africa and the UK, his work takes him across the world. He commented: "If we had known what was around the corner in 2007, people would surely have paid even more attention to your writing. This new edition draws us further into the world of work and how to succeed."

Chloe Charlton works at Morgan Stanley in the City of London. She wrote: "Strangely prescient – how did you know so many people would need this so much?"

Teresa Suttill is a director of a communications consultancy operating from the UK focusing on Latin America. She commented: "Some people might see this as a coach yourself kind of book. It actually goes further because it helps to instil the will to win and overcome adversity."

M Myilvaganan is a General Manager in Chennai, India. He wrote: "You have succeeded in making this creation light-hearted and at the same time it triggers one's thought processes. This book is for all seasons. However, it will be particularly helpful to balance our emotions and ease our mind, whenever we are under stress for some reason or other. This is a great effort from your side and I congratulate you for this work"

Margaret Kett runs the executive coaching practice at HADIL – Human Asset Development International Limited. She works closely with leaders in FTSE 100, 250 and entrepreneurial SMEs. She wrote: "Coaching is the enabler that ensures executives realise their potential through ever higher levels of performance. This book is a powerful tool, giving the reader access to messages that can enhance their abilities and strengthen their resolve; I have no hesitation in recommending it."

James McKechnie works in financial services and is a former Managing Director at Deutsche Bank. He commented:"This easy-to-read look at life should make people think. It will help them conserve what they have, help them stay sane and enable balanced enjoyment of all life throws at them."

The author remains grateful to all these contributors who have shown a remarkable consistency of view, whether they are from the Americas, Europe, Africa, Asia the Far East or Australia. It seems this work continues to strike a chord with a diverse community.

Preface

This is a collection of quotations and aphorisms about getting the best out of life. Some people see them as the embodiment of a philosophy, while others see them as an eclectic mix of amusing anecdotes.

They were collected over more than fifteen years, from experience in corporate life, through the trials of family life, at home, through leisure pursuits and through simple observation and listening to others.

It is meant to be light hearted — so please don't take it too seriously! But if it strikes a chord and helps in some small way, then I have achieved what I set out: to help improve people's experience of life.

If you are expecting lots of full colour photographs and illustrations, you may be disappointed. However my hope is that you will get far better pictures in your mind as you think about what is written here. My hope is that the value of this book lies in the debate you have with your inner self.

The quotations are not attributed — mainly because I did not collect the authors' details but also because I want the reader to focus on the quote rather than who said it. If I have inadvertently used your quote or your company's slogan, please treat it as free advertising!

Preface for the Second edition

When I completed the first edition of this book, it was early 2007. All was well in the garden of life for so many people around the world. And yet I knew something was going to give. Things could not continue unchanged. In addition, my work was not above criticism. Some people questioned its relevance as they took on yet more debt.

Five years on – and what a difference! Sub-prime mortgages, The Northern Rock, Lehman Brothers, The Euro, unemployment, empty shop units in the high street, Barclays. We now see massive de-leveraging of individuals, corporations and countries. It seems my thoughts anticipated a different world. A harsher environment of austerity rather than excess. As European economies faced financial restructuring one after another, I received more letters and even phone calls of encouragement. I had a call from the director of a firm providing elder care or "senior living." She told me that this would be recommended reading for staff.

I take no pleasure in observing the hardship that many people face in this post-Lehman world. No schadenfreude. Many "Fair weather" managers have been tested in adversity as profits halved (or worse) in 2009. Some did not survive and the face of the high street has changed in many countries forever. Yet those with resilience to keep going are the people I admire. Now more than ever, inner strength is a requirement for business and life success.

Whether you use this book for yourself, your family, friends or your work – your team, your organisation or just your next presentation, my aim is to provoke reflection on what really matters. I am sure that will lead to better decisions, more focused action and better outcomes. Even if you disagree with me completely – that is fine. My only request is that decisions are better informed by the occasional pause for breath in a fast-forward world.

Contents

Contents

Introduction

What? Another self-help, personal development, "coach yourself" book?

Not quite; this is a set of quotations and sayings from those who have inner strength already. They know.

Some of the quotations are simple and literal. Others are more complex with hidden depth of meaning.

You might like to think a little longer…..

I have therefore arranged this book so that you can use it in several different ways:

Firstly, you could read the quotations on the right hand pages and reflect upon them.

Secondly, you may want to read the narrative on the left hand pages to add colour to your thoughts or conversation if you are discussing these concepts with others (great at dinner parties I am told).

Thirdly, and totally for fun – you might want to open the book at random for instant comment. At one dinner party, my nephew started asking random philosophical questions and then opened the book. He then read out the quotation and we had a great laugh due to the surprising appropriateness. In any event it provoked lots of further fruitful debate.

Friends and relatives tell me that the value of this book comes from interrupting one's normal line of thinking. The quotations provide an uplifting challenge to our approach to everyday life. Friends also tell me that the quotations provoke real debate – enabling people to discuss topics that frequently are missed in a fast moving, transient world of ritualistic but superficial conversations. A pause button in a fast-forward world.

You might ask whether following the advice contained in the quotations diminishes spontaneity, fun, or freedom to be unpredictable? I would argue to the contrary – it is precisely by being in greater control and through having inner strength, that one has the power to decide. It can be very liberating to be able to say with confidence: "for once, hang the cost, we can afford it…"

The source material came from over 15 years of collecting quotations and aphorisms. They reflect experience, observation, the media and literature. Most of them had particular relevance to me when I first came across them. All have been discussed with friends who have understood real meaning in them. Some have even been kind enough to say that these few words can change lives. This is because they act as an insider's guide or "Indian Guide" to the trials and tests of life. From that point of view I regard them as small jewels in life's rich tapestry.

I hope they provide a source of additional strength and help to pump up your optimistic, cheerful disposition.

Or as a fourteenth century Samuri warrior once said: "No fear; no surprise; no hesitation; no doubt."

Ian Muir

Maó January 2007 and September 2012.

About the author

Ian is a director of Keeldeep Associates Ltd, a specialist advisory firm on top team development whose purpose is "surfacing effectiveness."

He works with senior teams and individuals to improve organisational and personal performance. He has worked across five continents and was previously an Executive Committee member at Charter International plc, a Director of Cable & Wireless International Group Ltd and a Trustee of a £2.2bn pension fund.

He is a graduate of Bath University, a Fellow of the Chartered Institute of Personnel and Development and a Member of the European Mentoring & Coaching Council.

An alumnus of INSEAD business school and a visiting Fellow of London Metropolitan University Business School, he has also worked with Ashridge researching the effectiveness of board evaluation.

Over a business career spanning more than 30 years, Ian has interviewed and coached people at all levels. He has been involved in leadership development, training of managers and coaching in the skills of influencing with integrity. Ian has worked in North America, Central America, The Caribbean, South America, Europe, Russia, The Middle East, India, Singapore, China and Japan.

His wife is an international linguist and interpreter who has provided invaluable insights regarding alternative perspectives on common issues. Cultural differences, once identified can bring deep understanding to different norms.

One of her favourite anecdotes is: "You English have table manners; we continentals have food."

Ian's observations are not confined to the business world. This collection of quotations comes from all walks of life, including people who are young, old, highly educated or just street-wise, employed and unemployed. The common characteristic is that the collected wisdom is from people who have all displayed inner strength, presence and calmness. Many have displayed great strength to overcome considerable adversity.

Similarly, the quotations and aphorisms have been discussed with people young and old alike – many of whom derived great value from the same quotation but for different reasons, in differing ways depending on where they are in life's journey.

These discoveries led Ian to explore the hidden rules of enjoying life. There are tacit and sometimes arcane behavioural codes but there are also unwritten rules of attitude and approach that help some people lead more fulfilled lives. The coaching value of this quotation collection has been helpful to those wanting a different, better, stronger perspective on life. You may find the quotations are somewhat repetitive in nature. However, those that may appear similar can have subtly different nuances and lead discussion in different directions. Many are systemically linked to each other and should not be viewed in isolation. They are part of a wide canvas. The author's purpose is therefore simple: to help others achieve a more cheerful, optimistic disposition, founded on resilience and strength.

Having left the corporate multinational life, Ian now works independently. He is also a valued speaker at leadership development events and conferences.

You can contact him at ian.muir@keeldeep.com

When not travelling for business, Ian and his wife Ingrid divide their time between England, Germany and the Balearic Islands.

The elevator to success is broken; please use the stairs

Many people grew up with their professional life making real progress in the 1990s and 2000s. Apart from a few cyclical fluctuations in the economy, the path was generally upwards. The old certainties remained exactly that – certain. Provided one performed well against demanding but achievable objectives, one's career remained a career. In family life too, there was evolution more than revolution. For some, the trade-off for being on the corporate treadmill was promotion and progression. This had come to be seen as the ultimate deferred gratification of western society. The good old final salary pension kept on accumulating.

Who would have thought 2007 would see the first run on a UK bank in nearly 200 years? The new reality came as something of a wake-up call for those who thought the trees would grow to the stars. It came as a shock for those who steadily borrowed more and more to keep up with the Jones's. And a tragedy for those who were tipped over the edge whether occupationally, financially or emotionally. People say it is a recession when other people are affected – but a depression when it affects you.

So these days we all have to be more realistic, more resilient and to break sweat a bit more. No longer the elevator to success. We have to get fitter and stay fitter by using the metaphorical if not the actual staircase. Knowing how to do things the hard way is an additional capability. More versatile skills at work are valued and flexibility is ever more important. Anyone can simply press a button, but achieving the goal in a more self-sufficient way shines more brightly these days. One consolation is that in the event of fire, we know how to get to and navigate the stairs! And that capability is a strengthening experience.

The elevator
to success
is broken;
please use
the stairs

Remember that not getting what you want is sometimes a wonderful stroke of luck

In the fast-paced, pre-Lehman collapse world with relatively easy credit, many people took a transactional approach to life, consumer goods, status and fun. Time was short and immediate gratification became a priority. When having what you want is relatively straightforward, not getting what you want is a source of frustration. In that fast paced world "I want it now" was the new mantra. Gone were the days when my father said "Of course you can have that attractive toy in the toyshop window. All we have to do is work out how many weeks pocket money it costs, you save up and after the required number of weeks – it's yours!" The value of this test of my resolve was that if while saving, I subsequently had second thoughts or found something better, I had not wasted my money.

My sister-in-law has an "iron law" regarding house purchase. It is this: everyone she has ever known, who has had a house purchase fall through – for whatever reason, has always ended up with a better one. I tested this but after some thought and checking, I think she is right. "Better" does not necessarily mean cheaper or higher quality – it means more appropriate.

So the danger of too much spontaneity is that it clouds our objectivity, prevents a more reasoned approach and stops us questioning whether we need something at all. Not getting what one wants can teach us a lesson, which ultimately opens up all kinds of hitherto unforeseen possibilities. The apparent adversity strengthens decision-making and broadens one's outlook. If you don't get the job you wanted, always seek feedback on how you can win next time.

Remember that
not getting
what you want
is sometimes
a wonderful
stroke of luck

Chinese proverb says
cow in field may not be all it seems

On initial inspection, this probably strikes you as pretty obvious. So you may think of "look before you leap" or "make sure everything is as it appears – don't be tricked."

To my mind, the bucolic agricultural context is interesting. Often, what can trip people up is not recognising something because it seemed so innocuous, so inconsequential. After all, what could be simpler or more obvious than a cow?

But in a busy life, it is the obvious that gets overlooked. So without becoming overly suspicious, it pays to check that things are as they appear – especially if they appear innocuous. That way, there is no doubt or hesitation – which means far fewer surprises.

Fewer surprises often reflect better planning and organisation as well as far fewer "Ah-ha" moments where some simple learnings can have great impact. Fewer surprises also reduce the stress of embarrassment on account of overlooking what with hindsight, now appears so obvious. Self-awareness and using colleagues to develop 360 degree vision is helpful in checking things.

Being prepared prevents problems. Expect the unexpected. And don't forget cows can also kick and stampede! If you do "put your foot in it" remember too that cows produce something less pleasant than milk.

In today's world of greater austerity, it pays to think twice. If something sounds too good to be true – it probably is.

Chinese proverb says
cow in field
may not be
all it seems

The glass is always half full, never half empty

This is one of the most well known debating points. However another twist on the concept came from someone who was shown an image of a half full glass and he was asked what it was. He replied "It is a glass that is twice as big as it needs to be." I find that interesting because it assumes that with a correctly proportioned glass, the contents would fill it completely. In a single statement, the idea has shifted from the ambiguity of half empty/half full to completely full – in an appropriately sized glass.

Now that is a positive outlook!

For me, the concept is about valuing what one has and then appreciating it. I have heard many people complain about share prices or the alleged value of possessions. I have often caused them to reflect silently by interrupting them and saying "well that's better than...." and then quoting a share price one penny less or a house price one pound less than the price they said.

My observation is that we tend to think things should only increase. "More is good." However the danger is that the great can become the enemy of the good. How many people have you met who are delighted with their car only to despise it when their friends turn up in something bigger, more expensive, more sporty or prestigious?

If one's resources are diminished – i.e. the glass is now only half full, think about the value of that – it remains better than a quarter full. If your business has shrunk, make the most of the new reality to grow again – better and stronger.

The glass is
always half full,
never half empty

Don't let a little dispute injure a great friendship

When we are very familiar with our friends and colleagues, it is sometimes easy to drop the social niceties of normal polite conversation. So when inevitably, differences do arise, friction can sometimes accelerate. Once such friction grows into an entrenched position, it can be hard to back down. The result is an inability to see the wider context of what friendship is all about.

The danger is that obstinacy or entrenched positions can be interpreted as uncaring and confrontational. And so a great friendship or effective cooperation at work gets damaged.

Perhaps there should be a decision point in any dispute, no matter how small, when each party asks themselves what there is to be gained by pursuing the dispute. There have been many legal cases where formal disputes escalated in time, emotional toll and cost – to a point neither party wanted to get to. Unfortunately, by then the stakes were so high that the disputes became self-accelerating machines that consumed people and their money. The news programmes frequently tell of court cases ending in astonishingly expensive pyrrhic victories.

Keep a sense of proportionality. Surely the very essence of a great friendship is that it can resolve little disputes? Or at least enable people to agree to differ. If not, then maybe it is not such a great friendship after all? This of course provokes some much deeper questions: what exactly is the nature of friendship? What is friendship and why is it important to people? What are the real tests of friendship and what are the agreed common strengths? Why do you value someone's friendship and what would you miss if it was gone?

Don't let a little dispute
injure a great friendship

Know the difference between having and living

I met a businesswoman once who proudly boasted that she was out every morning before 7am, had a very demanding job and got home at 9pm or later. She had a perfect Chanel outfit, Prada bag and Cartier watch but complained about needing a new cleaner. She also longed for her next Caribbean holiday. When asked why she needed all these expensive trappings of success, she eventually admitted they were rewards for the punishing schedule. I asked whether she would still need them if the schedule wasn't so punishing and she slowly realised that she was on an addictive treadmill. Maybe a diamond-studded treadmill ....but still a treadmill. In fact a great deal of her net income was spent on an expensive high-consumption lifestyle. And for what? No husband, no children, no long term friends — just lots of superficial acquaintances and contacts.

There is frequently a trade-off between earning and having free time but many people don't recognise the insidious creeping nature of the addiction. Yes it's exciting and tiring but the frequent flyer gold airline card too often becomes a divorce card.

I also met a very happy person who said that children are the reward for living. They had opened her eyes to the simple pleasures of life.

We all have to make decisions — whether to climb the greasy pole or not, whether to push harder for success. But make time for personal renewal. There is a balance to be struck. All the possessions in the world and no support network is the loneliest and most meaningless place on earth.

Know the difference
between
having and living

No life without wife

I like the poetry in this one. Of course it also implies "no life without husband" or "no life without spouse." The essence of this is the value of partnership, support and sharing life's journey. I have met many single people who appear content and have the trappings of success. But on discussing their lives at a deeper level it is frequently the case that there is something missing – a deeper sense of fulfillment is lacking.

Certainly, many single people have very active social lives, pursue multiple hobbies and are always busy. One said "I never was the pipe and slippers type." However I felt that the high activity levels were something of a displacement to avoid confronting the fact that they were alone.

I have also met some deeply satisfied couples who had an empathy (if not telepathy) whereby the simple life had its own attractions. They did not need to pursue an action packed social life – they had other priorities. The added dimensions that marriage had brought to their lives far outweighed the disadvantages and restrictions.

Of course the divorce rate is alarming and there are plenty of deeply unhappy couples and families. However marriage is still very popular and most people aspire to it. On a simple factual level, married people live longer and stay healthy longer. They also suffer fewer accidents. It also goes without saying that the ability to compare notes and seek sounding board advice has huge value.

No life
without wife

In the end the only people who fail are those who do not try

Giving up is a very negative path to follow. It affects all aspects of one's physical, social and economic life. Trying new things as well as trying to achieve familiar things are all part of our need for achievement. Naturally, we all want to succeed in what ever we do – but trying and failing is no disgrace. Remember: not getting what you want can sometimes be a remarkable stroke of luck. The learning that comes from trying and failing can lead to better solutions. Edison said that he was not discouraged by his thousands of attempts at making electric light bulb filaments. He once said: "I've just discovered the 1000th way of how not to make...." But when he got the design right, he allegedly said "I'm going to make electricity so cheap only the rich will be able to afford candles."

People who retain the right attitude and try – especially in adversity, frequently do succeed. They also tend to get noticed. Many employers are more interested in "attitude" than just qualifications or intellectual ability. Of course they want appropriately qualified and experienced people, but those are the minimum or "entry" stakes. What counts more and more are personal characteristics and the will to keep going – especially where this requires a change of direction. Getting noticed at work for endeavour is increasingly valued. More and more managers hire for attitude and train for skill.

Individuals who are not prepared to make some effort or to have a go at a result are quickly written off as "wasters with bad attitude." This may be unkind but that is frequently the perception: either consciously or not.

In the end
the only people
who fail
are those
who do not try

> If I accept you as you are I make you worse.
> However, if I treat you as though you are what you
> are capable of becoming, I help you become that.

This quotation is one of the longer ones in this book but it is worth spending some time struggling with it. Acceptance of people and their shortcomings tends to reinforce the status quo to the extent that people regress or go backwards. However given the right encouragement, they grow. By helping people to aspire to greatness – in small and subtle ways, one helps them grow. The first time I had a director's role reporting to the CEO I expressed some hesitation regarding a particular project. The CEO came close and simply said "We wouldn't have asked you to do this if we thought you couldn't do it." That was leadership and inspiration. In one fell swoop it said "we (not just me) have confidence in you, you are the right person to do this, it's OK to make a mistake and we will support you."

Another CEO summoned the board for a day on recruitment, succession planning, and talent management. Apparently he took out a wooden Russian doll – to the amazement of the board. In silence he slowly opened the two halves to reveal the slightly smaller Russian doll inside. He took it out and so on, and so on, opening up successively smaller dolls. At last he said "If you hire people who are smaller than you, I will have a company of dwarfs." He then re-assembled the Russian doll, again in silence, at last he said "If you hire and develop people who are bigger than you, I will have a company of giants." "Good morning." And that provided the instruction for the session.

If I accept you as you are
I make you worse.
However, if I treat you
as though you are
what you are capable of
becoming,
I help you become that

A loving atmosphere in your home
is the foundation for your life

This might appear simple, quaint and obvious. However, it is all too easy to let the frustrations of a busy day / week / month / year spill over into trivial arguments and corrosive comments. Over a period of time, such corrosion takes its toll – especially as most people have a repertoire of stock phrases. Repeated over the long term, these can damage a relationship. Or, to put it another way, irritations, frustration and stress can cause little disputes to injure great friendships – let alone love.

Emotional warmth and security at home are two of the most powerful weapons in the armoury of inner strength. They help people retain a sense of perspective. For example, people wedded to their work run the risk of putting too many emotional eggs in the occupational basket. Faced with redundancy – the sky sometimes falls in. By contrast, those with a stable foundation at home, more often keep a sense of perspective that says "it's a job, I have marketable skills and I can get another one – even if I don't get what I want, I have the support I need." I have seen many examples of people bouncing back faster and better after setbacks – where they have a loving atmosphere in their home as a foundation for their lives.

Partners have often provided the perspective of who the person is rather than defining people just by what they do. It is hardly surprising that when it came to redundancies, the financiers who fell furthest in 2008/09 were those who had introduced themselves as job title, bank then name. Even in social situations.

Emotional security defends against physical and economic adversity. It keeps you healthier and you live longer.

A loving atmosphere
in your home
is the foundation
for your life

Challenges can be like stepping stones or stumbling blocks; it is a matter of how you view them

We all face challenges and sometimes they build up. I like to think of a large Japanese garden, containing a lake with stepping stones across the water. Its serenity helps focus the mind. It can help if one thinks of the links between each challenge: if it is too great or appears insurmountable, break it down into smaller steps. After all, stepping stones are easier if they are not too far apart.

Think about the link from each step to the next. Keep a sense of agility – ie: don't waste time. And certainly don't stop or get paralysed. Remember, traversing stepping stones needs to develop a rhythm. If you stop you may become daunted by the expanse of water around you in the garden. So try not to stop in the middle of the stream and get bogged down.

If this all sounds too metaphoric, think about challenges in terms of how many perspectives and possible approaches are there? Which perspective is the most appropriate? Whose point of view has relevance? And why?

If you think in terms of a variety of different perspectives, you are half way to not just a solution but frequently the right solution.

Stumbling blocks are obstacles that block vision. Think about how to see around them. If you can't, ask someone else. And remember one person's stumbling block is another's stepping stone. Try to keep a sense of pace; this can be especially helpful in work situations.

Challenges can be like
stepping stones
or stumbling blocks;
it is a matter of
how you view them

Japanese proverb says
he who plants a garden plants happiness

At first sight, this quotation sounds very horticultural as well as intercultural! At a superficial level its meaning is reasonably clear: gardening brings happiness. However, I see a deeper meaning.

This says to me: if you plant or invest or spend money or devote your resources to anything, make sure there will be growth. In other words, make sure what you invest in – like a plant – can grow into something even more worthwhile. The opposite of course is don't devote yourself to things that shrink, degrade or depreciate. Or if you have to, make sure you understand in advance what you are doing and why. For example, many of us are seduced by fast or luxury cars, but how much are they worth after 2, 5 or 10 years?

This quotation also suggests one should derive satisfaction and inner strength from natural things rather than artificial things. The joy from nature is greater than the joy from conspicuous consumption.

Finally, it also says there is pleasure to be gained from waiting and growing something – by being patient, rather than pursuing spontaneous gratification all the time. For me one of the greatest pleasures has been the satisfaction of helping people grow. People who later said "You have helped me achieve things I never thought I could."

Understanding when and why one should devote one's resources to "planting a garden" instead of other things will ultimately provide a sense of economic strength and calmness because you will have wasted less and made wiser decisions.

Japanese proverb says
he who plants a garden
plants happiness

ABC: Appreciation before criticism

Apart from it simply being good manners, providing appreciation before criticism helps people to be much more receptive to criticism – and in a constructive way. There is good in almost everything – so there is no need to launch into criticism first. Doing that prompts a defensive reaction of denial or worse.

In order for people to be both receptive and amenable to taking corrective action, normally the ratio of "appreciation" to "criticism" needs to be about 3:1. In this way they are acknowledged for what is good and will then listen and take in how things could be (even) better.

Appreciation aids understanding of the various perspectives of the matter in question. Seeing the positive lifts your mood and aids healthy discussion. This helps put criticism into the right perspective: ie it helps prevent small negative aspects from overwhelming an otherwise noteworthy thing/item/situation/person.

I have found people to be far more committed to change and improvement when I said "These aspects are good because….and it could be better if these other aspects were as good too." Note the use of the word "and" – however tempting it is to use the word "but" – don't! "But" negates all that has gone before it. "And" creates the link back to what is good, helping to create aspiration.

Helping people to play to their strengths is always useful. Try asking someone: "When you are successful, how do you like to be acknowledged?" "Who would you like to appreciate your next success?" "How can I help them understand it?"

ABC:
appreciation
before criticism

Adversity elicits talents which in prosperous circumstances would have lain dormant

We all face adversity to a greater or lesser degree. But real adversity is testing and it's serious. True adversity tests one's physical and emotional stability, it also tests one's resolve.

On the basis that necessity is the mother of invention, one can see how adversity can bring hitherto unseen talents to the surface. Adversity invariably creates a sense of urgency and also focus. It helps to prevent distraction. So if your house is on fire, you will be focused on getting out and staying alive.

This antidote to complacency enables one to re-prioritise issues and see things with renewed clarity. There is an "adversity quotient" as a measure of capability in business. Some believe this is a better predictor of success than other assessment measures. The alleged reason is that drive for success and the ability to implement things – to get them done, are more important than many other factors. A CEO once said to me "If I had to choose between someone who was smart or effective, I would choose the effective person."

So don't give up when adversity rears its head. It is a test and for those who respond, it can help them to grow. Scary? Yes of course! Tiring? Naturally. But think about the lesser people who will give up, leaving you out in front.

Think also about the shadow you cast. You will be noticed for your fortitude. This will be remembered even if you don't succeed this time.

Adversity elicits talents which in prosperous circumstances would have lain dormant

The wise person has riches within themselves

This is taken from my father's school motto "The wise man has riches within himself." Wisdom has value and ignorance is costly in many ways.

While anyone can have an accumulation of material goods, wisdom cannot be taken away from someone. It therefore has a much deeper and longer lasting value. This is not to say that the wise person should not have riches as well. But the key point is that they have riches within themselves – which can also be put to use in a material sense.

A further consideration is that the value of wisdom can be applied to abstract matters, emotional matters and so many other things – not just materialism.

Riches without wisdom don't normally last. "A fool and his money are soon parted." Also, as an aspirational goal, wisdom is more permanent, more incremental and much broader than simply riches. The real enigma of course is can wisdom lead one to conclude that the pursuit of riches is a folly? In many cases it surely is because the addictive pursuit of material success has a tendency to cause blindness to what is really going on in people's lives. The pursuit of wisdom can extend into relationships whereas the pursuit of riches may not always promote the best in people.

It would be interesting to debate the relative value of material riches versus "riches within oneself." Clearly wisdom alone cannot pay the grocery bill. However the application of wisdom can enable better decisions and more rewarding jobs.

The wise person
has riches
within themselves

Life doesn't mean a damn until you can say "I am who I am"

This is about being at ease with oneself and not trying to be someone you are not. We all have faults and idiosyncrasies – learn to accept them and live with them. Clearly self-improvement is good but not in an obsessive way. People say "life begins at 40"; my observation is that this is the age when people accept themselves; the age when they stop worrying about how they might be seen or thought of. It is the time when people are more relaxed about who they are, what they have become – instead of aspiring for the unattainable.

People who are at ease with themselves learn that life does mean something. They are able to enjoy life, work and leisure with a healthy detachment from the anxieties of youth. Interestingly, by having this more relaxed approach, it frequently leads to greater self-confidence, self-esteem and influence. I have met many people who through their detached irreverence laid bare management gobbledygook, pointed out the emperor's new clothes or exposed the folly of obsessive consumerism. Such people have come from all walks of life: old and young, rich and poor, employed and unemployed. The problem is that climbing the corporate hierarchy tries to force us to define ourselves by what we do rather than who we are. Striving for authenticity is worthwhile, not least because independent thought is often highly appreciated at work.

I think that for most people, life has most meaning as well as enjoyment when they are not troubled by what other people think of them. A very self-assured person recently said to me "I don't need to impress people I don't know by spending money I don't have on things I don't need."

Life doesn't mean a damn
until you can say
"I am who I am"

Argue for your limitations and they are surely yours

Have you come across people who have essentially a negative approach to everything? "I can't do this, can I?" or "They wouldn't like us to do that, would they?" Such questions reflect an attitude of restriction not possibility. The assumed answer is "no" – so when it comes it is almost reassuring!

We have all met the "computer says No" response from poor customer service staff. I have met a number of people who when offered a suggestion, talk in detail about why it won't work, can't work, may not work, should not work or otherwise isn't working. Even when something cannot happen in its entirety, there is no sense of "let me tell you about how far we could go," or "let's talk about what we can do." Having a cheerful optimistic disposition opens up constructive positive debate. Frequently this leads to new possibilities, which overcome the small number of obstacles! So belief fosters creativity. Conversely, those who only argue for their limitations slowly but surely persuade themselves that nothing new is possible. And yet many of the great innovations come from ordinary people doing extraordinary things. This quotation therefore has a link to several we have reviewed already: adversity; the glass being half full and so on.

Those who argue for their limitations inadvertently develop a closed mind. I am not saying ignore constraints or the laws of physics – simply to challenge such thinking with "What if?" and "Why not?"

Argue for your limitations
and they are surely yours

Don't pay so much for something
that if it goes wrong you are traumatised

This quotation is about keeping a sense of perspective and balance. There is no point buying a £7,000 computer unless you can afford it. But how do you judge whether you can afford it? It might cost your life savings but theoretically you have the money. By contrast, if the amount represents two days net salary you might not think it is such a big decision. So how would you feel if the components failed and the technology became obsolete quickly? Guarantees aside, if you are traumatised by the thought, let alone the reality of a disaster with the product, then maybe it is consuming a disproportionate amount of your scarce resources.

Now let's think about the meaning of "pay" – it can mean more than money. You may want something so badly that you are prepared to give up a great deal in order to have it: money, time, relationships, other resources. I think the principle still applies: if you have to give up too much, then ask yourself why is it so important? When I have asked people "what is the most extravagant thing you have ever bought?" most have answered that "it seemed a good idea at the time but on reflection it was a waste."

My test of "would you be traumatised if it went wrong?" has proved invaluable for several people to moderate some of their excessive aspirations or decisions.

Don't pay so much
for something
that if it goes wrong
you are traumatised

The mind is its own place and in itself can make a heaven of hell and a hell of heaven

Or to put it another way "reframe the context." The mind can play tricks with emotions, judgement and rationality. The level of stress that people experience is the outcome of the pressure minus their individual coping mechanism. High pressure, higher coping mechanism = low stress. Low pressure, no coping mechanism = big stress. One's attitude and approach make a great difference.

I was once cycling in winter and suddenly it stated raining and hailing. My hands and face were quickly stinging in the heavy downpour. Within minutes I was soaked to the skin and getting very cold. The coping mechanism was to remind myself of an off-piste skiing expedition during which we experienced very high wind chill to about minus 40 centigrade. This was so extreme it made breathing difficult and skin felt as if it was on fire. Against that contextual thought, the hail storm was not so bad – in fact it was trivial and I hurried home to the bath.

Conversely, I know people who will seek out things to exaggerate and create anxieties about them. Almost all their worries are about things that don't actually happen; it is simply the thought or the possibility that is enough to create real anxiety.

Keep calm and carry on - the ability to re-frame the context is a valuable skill. It helps one address the situation with calm resolve – to get to a better outcome faster. It helps one avoid the paralysis that so often gets in the way. It also keeps things in perspective – after all I got caught in a hail storm, not a life-threatening blizzard miles from civilisation.

The mind is its own place
and in itself can make
a heaven of hell
and a hell of heaven

The less you think about your future,
the more certain it becomes

Most people miss-read this quotation. They see it as "the less you think about your future the more uncertain it becomes." So you might want to read it again! The implied assertion is that the certain future becomes one of inadequacy, poverty, unintended consequences and problems in general. So the way to avoid the certainty of a problematic future is to think about it and to plan for a better one.

An obvious example has to be financial planning: people who live for today and who run their lives on a financial knife-edge fail to secure their future. They therefore consign themselves to a retirement of relative poverty through inadequate provision. Another example relates to health — binge drinking in one's youth leads to liver failure in later life. But perhaps the real value of this quotation is to cause people to think about their complete life plan. Life is a journey and by thinking about the whole journey, one can plan for an ever better future. Naturally there are setbacks and contingencies are required. But by thinking ahead, most people have a better, happier, more secure future in almost every sense of the word.

I once met a thrusting young business type who was asked a slightly rude and rather forward question by a pensioner. "Why aren't you married yet?" The young manager replied "Oh I'm too busy with my career for that." So the pensioner replied (to their face) "Stupid idiot; if you had a wife, maybe you wouldn't have to work so hard. And she would support you when you realise your ascent of the greasy pole could end at the next redundancy programme!"

The less you think
about your future,
the more certain
it becomes

Invest in relationships with those you love

This might at first appear completely obvious "motherhood and apple pie." However the key word is "invest." For me that means spending time, effort, emotional capital and personal warmth. Acts of unconditional, spontaneous love and kindness help build relationships and strengthen them against the inevitable storms and tests ahead. Investment of personal warmth has great value because what goes around, comes around. The emotional security of knowing one is wanted and loved is beyond any form of monetary value.

And as with more commercial forms of investment, investing in relationships is necessary to keep them maintained. It is perhaps all too easy for people to take certain relationships for granted. This is a pathway to misunderstanding and drifting apart. Try to prevent being asked: "What happened to that simple glint of an eye that has less force than a snowflake hitting the ground."

So investment for upkeep and maintenance is essential. That way, the return is likely to be reciprocal emotional support. In turn this further strengthens relationships – enabling people to grow their inner strength. I once asked a lady who had a very hard life bringing up a large family with no steady income stream, how she withstood all the difficulties life threw at her. The reply came with assured certainty: "an impenetrable fortress of love."

Finally, remember that this type of investment doesn't cost money, but you do have to give from your very self. In doing this, my observation is that people glow in what comes back to them. But be careful, a promise broken was never really made.

Invest in relationships
with those you love

A bend in the road is never the end of the road, unless you fail to make the turn

Believe it or not, I have met some people who think this is about motoring. By contrast, it has helped many others to appreciate that there "is more than one way to skin a cat." I like this quotation because it contains several concepts: the futility of obsessively going in a straight line when there are clear indications to the contrary. Secondly, the idea that the road does not end and that there is always another route or way ahead. It may not be a direct route but it is still a route forward. Thirdly, the notion that not making the turn is an act of failure – and a pretty stupid one at that – given the rather obvious nature of the road's course. Fourthly, the notion of failing to make the turn suggests the notion of someone travelling too fast. Excessive speed means people are not taking in the surroundings, not "reading the road," not appreciating what is going on around them and even not seeing the signs (let alone reading them!). At work, it has profound implications for those who deliver results but in unacceptable ways. The "how" can be more important than the "what."

The quote therefore contains many hidden messages and has certainly provoked lengthy discussions across the dinner table.

Finally I like the concept of smooth agility: for me this creates an image of smoothly taking the bend in the road and coming out the other side in good shape, gearing up for the next path ahead. Negotiating bends with agility reduces stress and builds confidence and flexibility - which add to experience and strength.

A bend in the road
is never the end
of the road,
unless you fail
to make the turn

We take risks not to escape life
but to prevent life from escaping us

No one is advocating unnecessary or excessive risk taking but taking no risk at all is a path to boredom, lack of opportunity, skill and ultimately having nothing to offer. Taking sensible risks leads to personal growth – both through success and through failure and learning. In fact, many people agree that the learning from failure is more valuable and has immense benefit when applied to later challenges and experiences. I spoke to a senior headhunter once who was disappointed with the number of "fair weather" managers he had seen recently. He said "I want a Finance Director who has had to put a company into administration – that way I'll know she or he knows how and why difficult decisions need to be made."

Sensible risk taking is what life is all about. Managing those risks is a key part of learning, growing up and broadening one's capability. Whether it is learning to cross the road or ski a black run, both provide instruction. Perhaps we are in a new age of more sensible risk taking after the boom and bust of recent years. No one would advocate a 125% mortgage now.

Knowing where the boundary lies between responsible risk and irresponsible risk is a judgement call. More people will ski a black run than go hang gliding or free-fall parachuting. Interestingly, the more sensible risks one takes, the better one's judgement usually is – because of constantly pushing the boundaries of experience.

Life needs a little excitement but not to excess! After all, most adrenalin junkies come to a sticky end.

We take risks
not to escape life
but to prevent
life from escaping us

Insanity is repeatedly doing exactly the same thing
in the expectation of getting a very different result

Let's face it, we all get slightly obsessive from time to time.
There are however times to stop, step back and reflect. If
you keep bending the nail when you hit it with a hammer,
it might be appropriate to try another way, rather than
to keep wasting nails. At work, leisure and sometimes in
relationships, these repetitious tendencies show themselves
in different ways but almost always, if something isn't going
to work the first time, it won't work the tenth time. If
your business is not succeeding, sometimes substantial or
radical change may be required. Incrementalism may not be
enough and so a strong, brave response may be necessary.
The real skill of course is to approach the challenge from a
different perspective. Learning from errors and applying that
learning flexibly is one way forward.

Another aspect of this quotation relates to hectoring or
trying to persuade someone of something without giving a
compelling reason. Repeating "because I say so" rarely works.

Sometimes irrationality or greed causes us to do things
repeatedly. For example, if one has not won the lottery after
several weeks and the odds don't change, then maybe it is
time to stop playing because odds of 14 million to one mean
one really isn't likely to win in 100 years.

The message is therefore: be flexible, understand what you
are doing and why, be aware of irrationality and always be
prepared to step back and review. Armed with additional
perspectives, adaptation can then follow. People with
resilience have a skill in applying rationality in a confident
way.

Insanity is repeatedly doing
exactly the same thing
in the expectation of getting
a very different result

If you want to increase your success rate, double your failure rate

At first sight, this quotation may appear to be a complete contradiction of the previous one. Surely it cannot be advocating repeatedly doing what doesn't work?! Many experienced people would agree that success does not occur by accident – it is more the result of hard work. If failure leads to learning which in turn leads to success, then failing more should lead to more learning and more success. Perhaps the simplest example is in selling. If every 10th customer call results in a sale, then increasing the number of calls from 50 to 100 increases sales from 5 to 10. But the often ignored benefit is that the higher work rate or intensity can lead to greater focus – focus only on the things that matter to securing the sale. So the time pressure diverts effort preferentially to activities that win sales. And that raises productivity.

Learning from failures helps people to adapt and try different tactics. The real skill is to avoid repeatedly doing what caused the earlier failures.

For most people who have any sense of competitiveness, increasing the failure rate increases their resolve to do more and try harder. Now of course this can only be true up to a point. However, failing provides the most valuable information – used wisely it helps people to modify their actions and reach success. And always remember that much hard work is required to reach success. It rarely comes easily. Sustaining success in a rapidly changing world requires even more effort.

If you want to increase your success rate, double your failure rate

Things are going to have to change, in order to stay the same

Every successful business is two strategic decisions away from failure. I am reminded of a poster which had this slogan and a very close up image looking into the barrel of Clint Eastwood's gun. It used to hang on a colleague's office wall. The need is for constant reinvention – for business, for other organisations, for clubs and societies and for individuals. Career success is often predicated on one's ability to reinvent oneself to succeed in a new situation. This may be because one has a new job, a new boss or the work of the organisation has changed. Think about how businesses and brands have changed. For those who drove into London on the M4, 20 years ago there was a neon sign saying "Lucozade aids recovery." Today instead of tv adverts showing the Lucozade sick boy in bed, the brand positions the product as the ultimate isotonic sports energy fuel power provider.

Consider technology: first there were bookshops, then Amazon, now Kindle/ipad. We are probably in the last 5 years of universal print media. Digital growth is 200% a year while newspapers sell fewer copies every day. The British high street has changed: this is not just through recession with the demise of Woolworths and others. Photographic shops have gone due to the rise of smart phones. When did you last buy a roll of film? Have you ever? It is a similar story with CDs, card and toy shops as sales go online. Mass customisation and disintermediation are all around. Change is a constant; to stay in the running we have to reinvent ourselves for the new economic conditions. Riding the waves of change is strengthening. Only about 20 of the original constituents of the 1980s FTSE100 remain in it.

Things are going to
have to change,
in order to stay the same

From the moment you start earning, start building your "Go to Hell" fund

This came from a Professor at INSEAD, the business school. He said it was based on several pearls of wisdom: first, many young MBA students have a sense of confidence which is sometimes misplaced or bordering on arrogance. This can be a trap-door to failure if business relationships suddenly break down. Secondly, no matter how good you are, you should always try to anticipate the unexpected. Thirdly, there may come a time in your career when you need to make a stand – and dig your heels in for ethical principles. Having the will and the financial fire power to be able to do this is remarkably strengthening in every way.

While the anecdote was at first highly amusing – it provoked laughter in the amphitheatre, it subsequently provoked serious philosophical debate. Having an increasing measure of financial independence, even if it is only enough to withstand a short period of unemployment, builds inner strength. It stops people from being pushed around – psychologically and to a degree physically. This in turn reduces stress, increases confidence and enables people to speak their mind.

The strange thing is – that people who have that certain air of independence, who speak their mind without fear, frequently are valued for their candour – and for not being a "yes man." So the very act of building one's "Go to Hell fund" can actually reduce the likelihood of having to use it.

From the moment
you start earning,
start building your
"Go to Hell" fund

Have nothing in your home
unless it is useful or beautiful

Have you ever noticed that people are incurable collectors of junk? A recent cartoon of someone moving house had the caption: "Label all your boxes" The scene was one of hundreds of boxes all labelled "junk." Reducing clutter not only saves wasted expenditure but also makes for a tidier existence and a simpler less stressful life. A smaller number of longer lasting, well designed objects will be a smaller outlay but a much better return on investment than constantly buying replacements or unnecessary items.

I once met someone who needed to move house through lack of available space. They had allegedly outgrown their home. After the "mother of all spring cleans," they realised their house was actually perfectly suitable. Net result: a saving of tens of thousands of pounds.

Appreciating good design is a skill and source of lasting pleasure and calm. Of course, recognising that we are surrounded by bad design is also an affliction. But on balance, choosing fewer items that work well, will help make your home a haven of tranquillity. It is sometimes surprising how resilience is boosted by the experience of things working well and not letting you down. The satisfaction of a few great products usually outweighs the frustration of many where some simply don't do their job. In a stressful life, the coffee machine not working can cause people to hit it with a hammer! And a physically de-cluttered life often helps a mentally de-cluttered life. That means more focus, more clarity and more purpose.

Have nothing
in your home
unless it is
useful or beautiful

Hide from risk and you hide from its rewards.
Maybe hiding from risk is the biggest risk of all

Most of us are naturally somewhat risk averse. We put up our guard because deep down we believe the "safe" option really is the safe option. As the old saying goes: "No one ever got fired for buying IBM." But there is more to risk than simply playing safe. Hiding from risk means one does not learn to balance risk, appreciate sensible risks or take advantage of the opportunities that stem from risks. This goes for so many things in life: financial risk such as borrowing and investment decisions; relationship risk such as asking out your first date; even gastronomic risk such as trying a new wine! Someone once said the person who doesn't take risks probably makes two big mistakes a year.

And maybe it is true that hiding from risk is the biggest risk of all because it takes people into a cosy, unquestioning, easy path of avoiding all that risk can teach us. Complacency is dangerous – as we know, people with inner strength expect the unexpected. People and organisations that survive huge change tend to be those who are open to new ideas and who take risks. For example, photographic companies that experimented with opto-electronics brought early digital cameras to market. They were well placed for the digital revolution that swept film cameras out of the mass market. Those that licenced their technology to the mobile phone makers continued to survive.

The real value of this quotation though is its emphasis on the inevitability of risk – and therefore the unavoidability of risk. Once we accept that risk persists throughout life, it is simply a question of accepting it, adapting to it, working with it and learning from it all the time.

Hide from risk
and you hide
from its rewards.
Maybe hiding from risk
is the biggest risk of all

When in a stressful situation,
remember when and where you were happiest

This quotation is about re-framing context. We touched upon this in "the mind is its own place... hell of heaven and heaven of hell." People tend to exaggerate stressful situations and take an obsessively negative perspective. My observation is that few stressful situations are ever as bad or as stressful as they seem at the time. For example – ask yourself what is the worst thing that could happen? Usually you will say after the event "no one got killed and they learned from the experience."

In the heat of the moment, this may appear trite and easy to say – harder to do. So just reflect on when and where you were happiest: a favourite holiday, place, person, experience. This has a remarkably calming and strengthening influence that helps people to navigate their way through the stressful situation.

If that fails, imagine the source of stress in the widest possible context: if your employer fails or your wife/husband runs off – it is not the end of planet earth. Countless others have faced, withstood and become strengthened by their experience of getting through this. Almost all successful companies began by someone getting fired from another company.

Never be terrorised by anyone's terror. They can only terrorise you if you give them permission. An Asian colleague told me: You can hold a million grains of sand in your hands and there are more stars out there than all the sand grains on every beach on earth. Now just how significant is one angry person in front of you? Just think of them as shouting at themselves.

When in a stressful situation,
remember when and where
you were happiest

What would you do if you were completely fearless? And what is the first step you should take?

The concepts behind this quotation follow on from the previous one. I have used this when coaching people who have the right approach but who seem hell-bent on inventing things to worry about! It asks people to step outside themselves and to view the situation in a detached manner. Imagining themselves to be completely fearless, sometimes they can give surprisingly clear and direct advice. It is almost as if all manner of blockages are lifted.

The second concept is about fragmenting the advice into manageable chunks, then putting them into the right sequence. Or as someone once asked me "how do you eat an elephant? – one chunk at a time." So asking people about the first step that they should take is about getting to the first action that will overcome the fear that causes so much paralysis. Once the first action is settled, the next question of course is about the second action, the third... and so on.

Note the use of the word "should" in ...the first step you should take. This is designed to cause people to advise themselves in the context of what they know is the right thing to do but which they feel disempowered to do. If the quotation had said "will take" many people might stop there and say "but as I can't, I won't."

I like this quotation because it is very powerful in so many different contexts. I have seen it build exceptional resilience in people. It helps to remove limiting ideas and assumptions. It breaks down learned behaviours at work and it opens up possibilities. It has even enabled people to ask for a rise - and get it.

What would you do
if you were completely fearless?
And what is the first step
you should take?

It is easier to act your way into a new way of thinking than to think your way into a new way of acting

I like the inverse symmetry of this one. It is so memorable. There is and has always been a difference between thinking and acting. I have met a number of people who are good at one but not so good at both. I have also met a good number of people who want to change but seem to have an invisible block – some sort of threshold barrier that prevents change. Frequently they know what needs to be done but cannot get round to do it. It is as though their rational thinking processes are overwhelmed by some invisible inertia.

Summon the quotation! This is because procrastination tends to be the outcome of trying to think your way into a new way of behaving or doing things. Instead, stand in the future and ask yourself: "if I was an Actor, what part would I play? What would an Actor do? ...and what sort of lead would an Actor take?"

By "acting" one's way into a new way of thinking, it is almost like trying on a new piece of clothing – just for size and not for colour or style. It is safe, it is not a final decision: just try it on for size. Gradually, the behavioural drive will help one to think things through differently and to see things in a different light. So acting your way into a new way of thinking is actually easier and it gets easier still. If nothing else, the sheer variety of approaches will expose the folly of thinking alone, without following up with real actions.

And if all else fails, you might like to reflect on the notion that action conquers fear – a topic that we will return to later.

It is easier to act your way
into a new way of thinking
than to think your way
into a new way of acting

When in a hole, stop digging

This came from a management colleague who was listening to an employee complaining about something and who tied himself in knots. What is interesting is that the employee was so passionate, he failed to see where his passion was taking him. Had he stopped, stepped back and thought of three things that were significant, he could have made a far greater impact. Similarly, had he made a little time to consider making an understatement, that could have been even more powerful.

The imagery of this quotation is helpful because as one digs oneself into an ever deeper hole, one's perspective progressively and inexorably narrows and of course it gets harder and harder to get out of the hole!

The other concept is stop digging to devote your attention to getting out of the hole. All too often I have seen people get their priorities wrong. For example people with debt problems have been known to go to a debt consolidator, take out a loan and carry on spending! If only they would stop digging, they could curtail their expenditure to the absolute minimum – and I really mean the absolute minimum. That way the upward path starts immediately and gathers pace faster.

Finally, people who are in a hole and who don't stop digging become very visible to others. Their folly is evident for all to see. Conversely, those who are really committed to getting out of their hole attract admiration and support. The more they tell others about how they are going to get out of the hole, the easier it gets. Their public declarations require bravery but this builds strength and resolve. At work people who say "I have made a mistake; this is what I am doing to fix it" earn huge admiration.

When in a hole
stop digging

Meetings can be indispensible,
when you don't want to do anything

In corporate life, we all have to attend meetings. Meetings are vital for communication, creating shared understanding, for project management and all kinds of other great purposes. Don't get me wrong – I know how important they are. But most people go into meetings thinking that participation will be according to rational sensible rules and processes. Sadly human nature often gets in the way. We all know that we should start on time, keep to the agenda (it helps if there is one), stick to the point, have no private conversations, no interruptions or walking out of the room for calls. But participants should also consider whether they are being constructive, are they listening and will they agree conclusions and actions before finishing on time?

There is however a different dimension in which those with strength and resilience can make a contribution that takes meetings to a different level. They recognise that damage is done by people who constantly have to justify their point of view. If this happens, they haven't done the pre-work of stakeholder management. Similarly any ping-pong "agree/ disagree" routine needs a re-start of the fundamentals. People who are hell-bent on finding the flaw in an argument or who shout people down with "look...I know" have missed the point – which is to allow people to struggle with ideas and to build creatively on the discussion. This is far superior to a typical dialogue of the deaf. Jumping in at the pause doesn't help either. Time for reflection and thinking are crucial. Finally, watch out for people whose answer is not remotely close to the question being asked! Having the strength to challenge such behaviour will improve your meetings significantly.

Meetings can be
indispensible
when you don't want
to do anything

80% of something is better than 100% of nothing

Have you ever met people with designs for great projects, adventures or other grand designs? The majority of such people I have met frequently get no further than their ideas. This quotation therefore links into the one about it being the things we don't do that we regret. All too often one hears people say with a sigh "...of course I planned to write and publish a book – but all the commitments I had got in the way and then 10 years passed."

If the only way to way to eat an elephant is one chunk at a time, if only people would approach their grand designs with a proper plan, then piece–by-piece they might make some progress. And as you might expect, progress encourages further progress.

Ultimately it does not matter that the perfect goal was not fully reached – getting close achieves the fundamental result. I know some people who set their hearts on buying a holiday home in the sun. They researched the market and planned their budget: they set clear criteria. But somehow nothing was quite good enough and ultimately a lot of time and money were wasted. During the elapsed time prices rose and their dream home went even further out of reach. By contrast, some other friends took decisive action, accepted a whole series of compromises but they bought. Over the next 5 years they transformed their purchase turning it not just into a great place for superb holidays, but also a rapidly appreciating asset, which could also be used as a retirement home in later life. While its value subsequently fell, it never went below the purchase price. The real value was that of enjoying Mediterranean life and that was deemed to be without comparison.

80% of something
is better than
100% of nothing

If you aren't prepared to go out into white water, you'll never learn how to canoe

This came from a former boss of mine who had noticed a measure of reticence or caution. If one never "pushes the envelope" one never learns. Naturally in canoeing, the danger is that one can get very wet or even capsize. So the ultimate situation is doing an Eskimo roll or recovering an upright position in the rapids. Cautious people tend to become more cautious rather than less. So making mistakes and learning from them adds incalculable value to one's experience – provided one learns the lesson!

Developing and perfecting a skill always requires perseverance and endurance, if not a measure of risk. Facing up to the risk and evaluating it is a judgement we all need to know how to do. Taking balanced sensible risks – such as canoeing in a controlled environment, can add to our capabilities and confidence. Of course no one is suggesting you should go sky diving without a parachute. But avoiding the rapids and playing completely safe all the time means one misses what canoeing is all about.

Much learning comes from experience; and learning to take the inevitable knocks and to bounce back from them is a very important skill. The other aspect about canoeing is that frequently it is competitive. So learning to take competitive knocks and still come up wet but smiling and with a strong will to keep paddling – are very valuable indeed.

Having one's resolve tested, happens more frequently than most of us recognise at the time. Displaying bravery can be highly valued, especially at work.

If you aren't prepared
to go out into white water,
you'll never learn
how to canoe

Don't try to boil the ocean

This quotation follows on from the previous one. Have you seen great plans get off to a good start only for them to ebb away as the valiant people slowly realise that they have taken on far too much?

I like the image of someone with a large furnace or flame heater trying to boil an impossibly large quantity of water! To them, their endeavours are relevant, pragmatic and worthwhile. After all, if you want to boil something, heat it up. But they have a blind spot. That is the inability to see things in proportion or to take advice from others who may have tried before. If only they would seek guidance from others and make a more balanced judgement, they could see the need for a more planned, staged approach!

And before you think the quotation is stupidly impossible, consider how climate change, diversion of rivers for irrigation and other factors could help. There is more than one inland sea that has all but dried up.

People with inner strength tend to notice the wider context more than others, they make the linkages between things that other people don't see. They seek guidance and benefit from their networks. This gives them the inside track and makes apparently impossible tasks easier. Above all, they prioritise and aim for the achievable. Their objectives are SMART – specific, measurable, achievable, realistic and time-bound. We know this acronym from work but do we ever apply it outside work environments?

Don't try to boil the ocean

Success is a journey not a destination

I think many of us fall into the comfortable rut of thinking that our income stream will continue forever. Others may assume that once they have acquired the possessions they always wanted, they have "made it." The problem with short term materialist goals is that they are short term. "Things" can be taken away from you. Many of them depreciate in value over time. They also wear out.

The other side of "success" is not materialism — it is about relationships, support networks, contacts, knowing who to go to for advice and so on.

By recognising that success is a journey and then cultivating that journey, many people have realised that it needs constant attention, maintenance and vigilance. Success also needs judgement. So don't waste money on that brand new executive car, either buy one that is 18 months old or go for something cheaper and hire a limo when you really feel you need one. Warning: people with inner strength seldom feel the need to show off by turning up in a limo!

Success is also a relative journey: how much you want relative to others is ultimately your decision. I am sure you will learn to recognise that the meaning people attribute to success is constantly changing.

By preparing, planning, and still leaving room for spontaneity, one's journey to ever greater success can be long but rewarding. It should never be a flash in the pan and there is no complete stop destination.

Success is a journey
not a destination

Behold the turtle; he only makes progress when he sticks his neck out

This is a striking image of a turtle or tortoise slowly moving on land, carrying its heavy shell. And it really does have to stick its neck out to makes progress! As soon as it retracts its neck and limbs, it becomes a stationary object: just the shell, or so it seems.

There is a parallel for us here. We are unlikely to make progress by doing nothing. We are also unlikely to make progress unless we are prepared to take some risk, be inquisitive, look ahead, extend ourselves physically, do some lifting and generally take the strain.

In English the phrase "sticking one's neck out" refers to taking some risk, being bold, visible and also having the confidence to proceed.

The turtle or tortoise, at first sight appears the least likely animal to take a risk or be bold. Normally they are very slow cumbersome, low-energy beings. But they also demonstrate a certain resolve and a dedication to travel inspiring distances, despite their slow pace.

There is another proverb about the hare and the tortoise. It is interesting that the tortoise wins the race – through consistency and persistence. And maybe that is where the depth lies: the moral of the story being that no matter how daunting a situation or problem may appear, by sticking one's neck out and taking the strain, one can make progress. Slowly but surely results, even spectacular results can be achieved.

I am told the world distance record for a turtle is a journey of many, many thousands of miles.

Behold the turtle;
he only makes progress
when he sticks his neck out

Cultivate friendship; you cannot buy with gold the old associations

There is nothing wrong with aspiration, ambition and application to get what you want. For many people, the attainment of a certain standard of living is their definition of success. However some people pursue this to their cost because they neglect the requirement to invest in relationships. They (wrongly) think that by devoting all their efforts to material success, that is enough. In the short term, it may be. However over the long term, this type of behaviour gets in the way of success – which I believe is mostly achieved through people and relationships.

We have all heard the phrase referring to someone who "knows the price of everything and the value of nothing." Or alternatively, "all the gear and no idea." These refer to people who have an imbalance in their approach. By valuing friendship and long-term associations one can retain a sense of perspective on what has real lasting value in life, not just transient pleasure. After all, today's brand new car is eventually tomorrow's rust-bucket.

The other aspect about the "old associations" is that they are the good will, the spontaneous help that other people provide. Sometimes when asked, sometimes unsolicited – but always willingly. And you really cannot buy this good will with gold. It is about the relationship bank account. Yes we all "overdraw" from time to time, but re-investing in relationships rebuilds that emotional capital. Discretionary extra help from others is beyond value. It can get you another job and even save your life.

Cultivate friendship;
you cannot buy with gold
the old associations

Look up. Depressed, stressed people look down and retreat into themselves physically. Adopting an outward facing, upward looking demeanour brings instant strength

This is strange but true. My observation of depressed people is that they invariably look down – if not quite chin-on-chest. I guess it all relates back to the foetal protective position of adopting a closed, "small as possible" protective posture. But by adopting an upward-looking posture, with chest slightly out, there really is an uplifting effect. If you combine this with thinking about when and where you were happiest, it can be a powerful strengthening tool in stressful situations.

My observation of people with inner strength is that they frequently look up and appear to project themselves with quiet confidence when in very stressful situations.

Light also helps. If there is light above (such as when you are outdoors) or even room lighting, this is better than staring at the floor or your shoes. Most people have heard of SAD or seasonal affective disorder. Getting out into the light is helpful. So think about taking a break at lunch time – however short, to get out of your building, look up and experience a different environment.

I have met people who say they don't have time to do this or even don't have time for lunch. (Allegedly not even 5 minutes) Many of them have come to a sticky situation because they had lost so much sense of perspective.

Look up.
Depressed, stressed people
look down and retreat
into themselves physically.
Adopting an outward facing,
upward looking demeanour
brings instant strength

The response is your communication

It is surprising, the number of times one can say or write something and get a very unexpected reaction. It could be from inappropriate wording, or body language or even the use of capitals in an email (which is regarded as shouting.) So the solution is to treat all one's communication as "receiver-driven." Consider what response you want and carefully tailor the communication with the response in mind.

Instead of being surprised by an unexpected reaction, listen carefully and try to understand why it is this way. Those with inner strength learn from these lessons.

Frequently, a better understanding of context can help one to tailor one's communication in a more readily digestible way. So ask some questions before giving the message. Having delivered the message, note the response carefully: that is the real message. And if it is not quite complete or correct, clarify it until the reaction is appropriate. Plan your communications in terms of what you want people to think, how you want them to feel and what you want them to do as an outcome.

A manager was making someone redundant. The company situation was so well known, he thought it perfectly straightforward to launch into the "you are redundant so here's the deal" conversation. Thankfully he had the good sense to check the employee's understanding. By asking some contextual questions it became clear the person had no idea the axe could fall on them. The manager immediately changed approach, building a simple clear explanation of why the department faced some extreme choices. When the response came it was far more measured and understanding. The employee thanked him for his candour.

The response
__is__ your communication

Accept that almost nothing goes according to plan; always have a "plan B" and "plan C"

There is a great deal of frustration caused by things not going to plan. Time after time, I see people getting irritated, annoyed or overtly angry at things not going right. This is no-one's fault – just circumstances or things beyond their control. The funny thing is, many people remain unaware that actually nothing ever goes according to plan. There are always twists, variations and changes. Some of them of course are fortuitous and very welcome strokes of luck. We often tend to forget those however!

Let's concentrate on what goes wrong. Timing, lost opportunities, other people letting you down, adverse conditions, costs increasing. All these things conspire to prevent what you want from going to plan.

The answer lies in having a "Plan B" and a "Plan C." Effective people have already thought through their Plan B and C – so when the (almost) inevitable happens, they move swiftly and apparently effortlessly to the Plan B. This does not just apply to corporate strategy, it applies to many simple things such as queuing at a shop counter (invite your spouse to hold a place in another queue line).

The more one can reduce surprises and frustration, the calmer you will be. Of course, the calmer one is, the greater one's reserves of inner strength with be too. Most people can get used to the idea of a "Plan B" but go further: "Plan C" and "D" are perfectly achievable even if only in outline.

Accept that almost nothing
goes according to plan;
always have a
"plan B" and "plan C"

Be a first class version of yourself rather than a second class version of someone else

In group or team situations it can be entertaining to observe how certain characteristics of the leader are copied. Maybe people seek the reassurance of affinity or tribal association? Many times, I have seen people adopting modes of personal appearance, dress, work style, ways of communicating and speaking. As a test, and actually for fun, I have introduced new words into organisational or team work only to see them adopted and used back on me with passion and emphasis! The next time a new senior leader arrives with a very short or long haircut, watch the hair styles among his/her senior team over the next 6 months! When new phrases are introduced, note who copies them first!

But in the end this is a little sad. Those with inner strength don't need to copy others. They are sensitive to the situation and would not turn up in an investment bank dressed for a building site! But they don't need to copy someone else. They have the strength to be different, to be themselves.

Be a first class version of yourself. Be clear on what you stand for and why. Be consistent, have a personal "brand" for which you are known. By being distinctive, you will stand out rather than be known as a "clone" of someone else. If one is in danger of being regarded as a copy of someone else, take care. When that other person goes out of favour for whatever reason, where does that leave you? From Roman times to the FTSE100, when leadership changes, management teams are judged.

Be a first class version
of yourself rather than
a second class version
of someone else

Try to acquire "hindsight from the future"

For me, this is one of the most fascinating of all the quotations in this book. Many people struggle with its meaning and it does require some thought. I have used it when helping people to think through many situations.

Here's how it works: when presented with a problem, think it though and discuss possible solutions. Then explore how those might play out and what the reactions could be. Think through the various outcomes to the plan. Then standing in the future, ask yourself "does this feel like the right place to be?" or "Is this exactly where I want to take us?" If the answer is "No," then while still standing in the future, give yourself the benefit of the hindsight you have acquired and ask yourself "knowing what I now know, what would I have done differently?"

Then rewind the film, go back to the present and re-plan your solution using the benefit of "hindsight from the future." I have heard many senior leaders say "mmm...I don't think we'll do that then..." as a result of them thinking through every step of a plan in this way.

This may sound simple but it takes skill and application. It is a technique that has proved very valuable, especially when used in conjunction with some of the other pieces of advice, such as having a Plan B and Plan C.

Used correctly, this has led to some very powerful and influential conversations that have completely changed initial plans and averted significant stress later. All of which contributes to inner strength.

Try to acquire
"hindsight from the future"

Don't create unnecessary work

This may seem obvious but it is worth exploring. In a pressured world with too little time, it makes sense to reflect on the value and appropriateness of one's actions. I once saw a notice at someone's desk that said "No I am not stressed and late, I did it right first time."

Some people in their quest for completeness or detail, sometimes pursue too much — such as making endless copies or mitigating risks grossly out of proportion to their likelihood of ever arising.

Even at home, have you ever observed some people in the kitchen use twice as many utensils as others? Or they make endless lists on small pieces of paper, only to lose a key scrap and waste 10 minutes finding it again?

The moral of this story is to do the right thing and not excessively the right thing. It is also to think ahead and to take actions that can be regarded as "no regrets first moves." What I mean by this, is — in a changing and uncertain environment, what steps can be taken which we would not regret later if there was a slight change of plan?

This doesn't just apply to business; almost every aspect of life can benefit from this. For example if you are going on a leisure trip but might get a call to attend to a sick relative, it makes sense to go to local attractions or those in the direction of where you might need to go suddenly. Lean thinking has much to teach us: it started in manufacturing but applies also to services and behaviour.

No one likes un-doing work or having to do additional activity — the more we can contain this, the greater our reserves of inner strength.

Don't create
unnecessary work

Set personal goals with check points along the way

This quotation links to others on the subject of "one chunk at a time" and not trying to boil the ocean. Yet it is surprising how often we launch into something big and don't know how well we are progressing. This does not just apply to simple tasks such as saving for a rainy day, it also applies to the strength of relationships.

I came across "If you don't know where you are going, you'll probably end up somewhere else" when I was a teenager. It had a powerful influence as I could see fellow A level students aimlessly drifting through their course not knowing what to do next. Some went to university with no particular objective in mind; others got caught up in more problematic activities and ended up aged 40 in low skilled jobs – wondering why they hadn't used their education more.

We can all set personal goals: for career, family, personal happiness and financial security. By having check points along the way, one can monitor and measure success but above all, take corrective action when required to keep on track. And of course, if the required corrective action comes as a real test of one's resolve: so be it! Let there be such a test and one should make the decision on the appropriateness of further action. It is better to take the decision (either way) rather than to drift. As we will discuss later, those with inner strength "happen to the world" – the world does not "happen to them."

Time and again, my observation of resilient people is that they have a plan, measure their progress and take appropriate action.

Set personal goals
with check points
along the way

Arabic proverb says: after lunch rest a while, after dinner walk a mile

This is interesting although I doubt whether the rhyme exists in the original Arabic. First of all the quotation provides guidance for weight control and exercise. It is well known that eating a large meal late in the evening is bad for the waistline. If you are sleeping while digesting, most of the calories are not burnt. Similarly, by going for a walk, the exercise raises the metabolic rate to burn calories during and after digestion. In any event exercise is good for you.

In hot countries resting a while after lunch is making reference to a siesta but it also says that constant work is draining and denies the opportunity for social interaction.

The gastronomic point may also be metaphorical. Could it be that after a "feast" in the middle of something – such as a mid year reward or bonus, one needs to pause and reflect. But upon completion of the day's work or the major project, one needs to redouble one's efforts ready for the next activity. The point here is the avoidance of creeping complacency.

I think the value of this quotation is concerned with avoiding complacency at any level. For example: achieving a balance of diet, exercise and getting the timing right. By looking after one's physical well being, there is a solid foundation for doing all the other tasks we have to do. By avoiding complacency we stand a far greater chance of succeeding when asked to do them.

Arabic proverb says:
after lunch rest a while,
after dinner walk a mile

Don't worry about things you cannot change

Many people worry too much. Maybe it is fear of the unknown or simply fear of what might happen. But even if something is certain to occur and it is a legitimate cause for worry – if you cannot change it then you need to work very hard to stop worrying about it.

This may be a tough challenge but worrying about things you cannot change saps your energy, reduces your reserves of strength and actually impairs your health. So if the cause of your worry is certain, worrying about it is worse than pointless because you will need all your reserves of health and resilience to address it head on.

Remember the pilot whose textbook emergency landing on the Hudson river made worldwide news. By having a calm and balanced emotional state, it is surprising how much better one can address the problem. This in turn invariably leads to a better, faster, more palatable solution than would have occurred had one been in an anxiety state! The recording of the dialogue between airliner and air traffic control is now used in training courses the world over. The problem with worry is that it is paralysing and debilitating. Some people worry precisely because they are certain something will take place and precisely because they know they cannot do anything about it. I say it is exactly because you can't do anything about it that you must not worry. Instead: do what you can to address the issue!

Those who prevaricate lose opportunities for mitigation and almost always end up with a sub-optimal solution. People who at least try to address the situation will make some progress, however slow. Denial simply does not work.

Don't worry
about things
you cannot change

Never get into the position of being only three payslips away from financial disaster

In our fast-paced "live-for today" spontaneous-gratification world, most of us want immediate satisfaction and some think they have a right to have it all now.

Maybe this was a by-product of easy credit when it was easy to borrow money and run up substantial debt in the UK and many other countries. With so much emphasis and peer pressure on having things, it is hardly surprising that there is pressure to spend, spend, spend. After all, everyone can see what you wear and drive; no one can directly see the size of your debt.

Our culture tends to assume that income streams will continue without interruption onwards and upwards. In the dot com bubble of 2000, commentators spoke constantly of "the new economy." That was before the crash and economic nuclear winter in the technology sector. With wider austerity across the world, more people now see the folly of such assumptions.

So never get into the position of being three payslips away from disaster. Put money aside in proportion to the real risk of income failure. That way you can sleep easy, knowing that you can ride out a storm, should one arise. Having economic strength also enables one to keep a healthy independence: you can speak your mind without fear. My observation is that "yes men" are those who simply cannot afford to miss a single payslip. Economic strength brings inner strength – fewer and fewer people can push you around if you have money behind you. Strangely, the more financially secure people become, the greater their inner strength and the less likely their financial and other reserves are ever called upon.

Never get into
the position of being
only three payslips away
from financial disaster.

Furnish your home with the minimum necessary, then half it

I think this came from Charles Rene MacIntosh. It is not a homage to minimalism; more a recognition that people are like squirrels (or pathological hoarders). Try this test: go into any retired person's home and ask yourself "is there too much furniture and other 'stuff' in this house?" The chances are that your answer will be yes. This is because we accumulate and fail to recognise when we have too much.

There was once a TV show called "life laundry" in which people had their homes (and lives) cleared of all the built-up clutter of the years. The de-cluttering started with physical items and then progressed to the occupant's psychology. There was however a serious message: don't let clutter build up in either your physical possessions or your mental and emotional state.

At a practical level, by having a house furnished with the minimum, it forces you to be selective, to go for quality and you know you will use what you buy. In that way it helps save a great deal by avoiding waste. Having this approach also makes your home feel bigger than it is – and that can help avoid the biggest expenditure of all: moving house to a bigger one. Have you ever noticed how when you move into a new home it feels big but after a few years it no longer does? And we aspire to a bigger one…..

The essence of inner strength is the ability to resist pressure to buy the latest of everything. I am not advocating being a Luddite, but simply to stop, think, and then decide in an informed way.

Furnish your home
with the minimum necessary,
then half it

You can't stop snow but you can learn to ski

This quotation is included to demonstrate that there are many ways of mitigating against discomfort, inconvenience or other uncontrollable problems. Also, one can re-frame the context and turn an apparent problem to one's advantage: hence the inconvenience of snow can be turned into a premium activity: skiing.

No matter how inevitable a problem or issue may be, there may be ways of not just coping with it, but positively flourishing with it. So instead of going under a wave of change one can try and ride the wave of change.

A real skill is the ability to recognise that an inconvenience or a problem situation can be put to good use under a different context. Many of us have great difficulty in seeing the potential of a challenging tough situation. Remember the Chinese character for dilemma includes the concept of both "crisis" and "opportunity."

The quotation is all about change and agility: if changing seasons or climate bring unexpected snow, then those with inner strength put it to their advantage by learning to ski – and maybe some will become ski instructors! This is of course allegorical – the expression could just as easily say: "You can't stop redundancy but you can retrain or you can develop a career as an outplacement specialist..." or "You can improve your chances of securing a new job through extensive networking and by cultivating that network throughout your career." Or even "You can't stop rain but you can shelter under appropriate clothing."

You can't stop snow
but you can learn
to ski

Laughing is medicine, see the funny side and things get better

Being able to see the funny side of things helps us maintain a sense of healthy detachment. Without going into a discussion on the medical benefit of endorphins, when you think about people who can laugh at the challenges of life, they tend to be happier, more balanced people. They don't face any fewer challenges, it is simply their way of dealing with them that is better.

There are also many medical studies that have found laughter helps one's metabolism and general health in a number of ways. By helping to reduce stress, laughter prolongs life span. Seeing the funny side of a difficult situation really helps one to see a much wider perspective. The benefit of a wider perspective can help you find new ways to solve issues or more creative ways of addressing frustrations. As with so many things, balance, breadth and a wider sense of context are frequently the route to better solutions, lower stress, greater confidence and strength.

If nothing else, seeing the funny side of a situation helps one to stop focusing only on the negative aspects. My observation is that when faced with a difficult decision or situation, many people tend to talk themselves into an increasingly negative frame of mind. Laughing about the funny side lifts the mood and creates a more constructive mandate.

Looking back, people have a tendency to remember the funny side and ignore the stress — so improve your own library of funny memories by concentrating on them closer to the time an issue arises. And try to remember them.

Laughing is medicine,
see the funny side
and things get better

Don't bet the shop

This quotation has been around for a long time but I think it needs re-emphasising in today's "I want it all and I want it now" world. We have already seen the importance of never being three payslips away from financial disaster. And yet some people persist in taking enormous risks such as multiple house mortgages, excessive short term loans, or debt consolidation at exorbitant interest rates. At a relationship or emotional level, people who fail to invest also run risks – emotional break down or unexpected divorce. The strain of this can be long term to say the least.

There should rarely be any need to take a risk with the bedrock of one's family, income, house and so on. "All or nothing" approaches tend to lead to the "nothing" outcome.

So the time to take risks is when you can afford to lose. As the stock market pundits say: "Never invest more than you can afford to lose." This is sound advice that could be applied to areas beyond the financial.

Another aspect of not betting the shop is that if one could see the underlying value of exactly what "the shop" is or means, then one might not be so silly as to consider putting it at risk. People who have "lost the shop" nearly always say afterwards "I must have been mad – if only I had appreciated what I had and how fundamental it was." Clearly they could have done with a dose of hindsight from the future – which could have saved the day. What stands out about people with inner strength is their ability to recognise situations for what they are and what they could develop into.

Don't bet the shop

De-clutter your life, ask yourself what is really important

This is all about the importance of focus. Most of us have a tendency to collect and accumulate not just possessions, but all kinds of trivia both physical and mental. In a busy life of "rush rush rush," there is little time to make decisions as we are driven by spontaneous immediacy. So when shopping, if there isn't time to choose between red shoes or blue, we buy both on the plastic. I like the de-cluttering advice that says A) Put everything you have not worn or used for a year into black plastic bags. B) Tie them up and put a label on them. C) Under no circumstances write the contents on the labels. Instead write a date on the label by which if you have not re-used the contents, they go to the charity shop or tip.

You are allowed to feel the exterior of each bag over the coming period of time – to determine whether you really want to re-open it. Some people are reluctant to name the future date – so I say "OK let it be another year. Or two." The aim is to force people to get more out of less.

In relationships by focusing on quality, the rewards are far greater. So set priorities and go for quality. I am not advocating the end of networking – not at all. But I am advocating conscious decisions to invest in quality relationships that matter and to use networking for its proper purpose. It is a folly to confuse the two and I have met some exceptionally empty people who had hundreds of acquaintances and a large Facebook presence but few real friends.

De-clutter your life,
ask yourself
what is really important

Listen to what your body tells you;
if you don't – who will?

This quotation comes from a former work colleague who had a health problem and yet looked the picture of health. However when people were driving themselves into the ground, she was one of the few people who could really see what was going on. Hence the advice. It has remained relevant because men in particular are so reluctant ever to see a doctor! They tend to think their bodies are like a car: if something goes wrong you simply get it fixed or fit a replacement part. The concept of mortality never enters the mind. We think we are invincible and immortal in our 20s and 30s.

If people could listen to and see the first signs of fatigue, illness, stress and so on, they could maybe do something about them pre-emptively. A breast cancer survivor once said to me "Looking back, I can now see the exact time when it started. I could not see it then but I do now. I was working very hard, flying all over Europe, 5am starts, 9pm getting home – if at all. I started feeling very tired and just could not shake it off. That was the start."

People with inner strength listen to their bodies and take note. They are far less troubled by the worry of illness because they know what is going on – and seek medical help as soon as required. But strangely, it tends not to be required so often because they already lead healthier, more balanced lives. They remain resolute: health comes first because without that everything else becomes more difficult.

Listen to what your body
tells you;
if you don't – who will?

Know when to stop

This is about recognising situations and knowing when to stop pursuing the unattainable, stop arguing, stop wanting more, stop being satisfied with poor performance, stop accepting injustice and so on. It is not just: "stop, you have enough" it is also "stop accepting second rate and take action."

The common theme is about knowing when to stop. This is a difficult skill to master and something of a never ending journey. But recognising the "game over" moment can be very helpful in negotiations, in consolidating what you have and in creating the drive for ambition.

We have all seen the person who is blind to their "flogging of a dead horse." It is awkward, tiring and embarrassing. We have also seen the person who simply won't let go in an argument and simply has to have the last word – no matter how damaging it is to a relationship. I have also seen people push too hard in business and "blow the deal" because they were too greedy, such as where a salary negotiation ended in the written offer never coming.

Knowing when to stop is about recognising situations, seeing them from an external perspective. Try to stand outside yourself and in an imaginary way, look back at yourself as an impartial observer. What advice would you give yourself and why? What is the next move and what could go wrong? Inform your plans and actions with a second opinion.

Know when to stop

There is no such thing as an outcome in an absolute sense

At first sight this quotation can appear deeply philosophical and also patently wrong. We all die, after all. But thinking further, one could start arguing about someone's legacy and their enduring influence on their family, their community or even the world.

In a more down to earth context, when decisions are made that one does not like, there may be elements of compromise or alternative ways to achieve a more acceptable aim. I am not advocating subversive tendencies in the workplace, community or family. However, outcomes are rarely absolute in perpetuity. For example how many times has a rule been made only for a few exceptions to be allowed, once the rule makers fully appreciated the unintended consequences of a blanket decision?

So don't be disheartened by adverse decisions. They are what they are but every cloud has a silver lining. And as we have seen earlier, sometimes not getting what you want can be a remarkable stroke of luck.

When one has an appreciation of there not being outcomes in an absolute sense – this helps one's resolve and patience. Or, to quote George Harrison the former Beatle "All things must pass." So adverse situations and decisions rarely persist for ever. My observation is that people with great resilience know this and are prepared to play a longer game and not be disheartened by short term setbacks. In the end, everything will be alright. If it is not alright, it's because it is not yet the end.

There is no such thing
as an outcome
in an absolute sense

The more you learn of other cultures, the more balanced will be your view of your own

One of the benefits of being married to someone who does not carry a British passport is the constant inter-cultural learning. I find it fascinating, that having been brought up to believe the BBC was the one and only truth of broadcasting, other broadcasters take a very different and equally plausible approach. Try this for yourself: if you have access to multiple satellite TV channels watch out for syndicated news footage of one particular news item. I have seen the identical footage (2 mins) edited into at least 5 different 60 second montages, with the story and voice over ranging from one opposite to the other – and all based on the same images!

Without wishing to take sides, this does help one to learn more about other cultures and why they hold the views they do. The world as we see it - is only the world as we see it. On the basis that context is all, an understanding of other cultures really does inform understanding of one's own.

The value of this greater understanding is that one can then see things that other people cannot. This enables one to achieve more, faster, better. It also helps one to influence situations to reach better outcomes – because you have a greater overall understanding of what is going on and why. It reduces the incidence of surprises and unforeseen outcomes – those "where on earth did that come from?" moments. In our globalised world of work, this understanding is a key differentiator. It promotes effective team working across work groups both locally and those that are dispersed.

The more you learn of
other cultures,
the more balanced will be
your view of your own

There is nothing permanent except change

This comes from ancient Greece, which just goes to show how wise they were. I think human nature is inclined to believe the status quo will continue indefinitely. Few people expect the unexpected. Most people think their income stream or bonus stream will continue uninterrupted. And yet change is the one great certainty. It is important that we all learn to cope with it, work with it, expect it and embrace it. It will not go away, ever.

Trying to return to the "good old days" simply does not work. In any event, our memories are selective and they progressively cut out the difficult parts. Perhaps the reason why people say school days are the happiest days of your life is because they forget all the childhood terrors and playground bullies.

By expecting and anticipating change we can prepare for it – which makes it far more acceptable and enables our psychology to approach it with a constructive opportunism rather than trepidation. As we will see later, chance favours the prepared mind. By being ready for change, we deal with it far better and are better equipped to seize its opportunities.

People with inner strength focus on the opportunities of change and they recognise that mostly, change is for the better. Consider how much more choice we have today compared with twenty years ago. Of course there are disadvantages but ultimately we do have more choice. If you want to retreat to a haven of tranquillity, it might not persist in the way you originally planned or wanted. As always and throughout the millennia - the future will surprise and it will be different.

There is nothing permanent
except change

Remember that silence is sometimes the best answer

...Or as my wife says "remember that no answer is also an answer." Silence can convey many messages. First it commands attention. Have you ever noticed that no one falls asleep through silence? Secondly it can convey a diplomatic sense of not wishing to say something difficult or even offensive – but everyone knows what could be said that is not being said. This can be a very powerful and memorable use of understatement. Thirdly, it can convey an enigmatic sense of mystery – that keeps people guessing about how much remains unsaid. Some people may assume there is more to this than there really is. Let that be a matter for them.

People may choose to interpret your silence in several ways but the overriding message is the fact of silence – there was no verbal answer.

Certainly, the use of silence can be far more powerful and influential than an answer that is inappropriate. Calm people rarely resort to rude or abusive language – all that does is open a contest to see who can accelerate confrontation fastest. The careful use of silence retains the higher ground. By remaining strong and in control, one reserves that high ground and occupies it.

I think the circumstances when silence can be the best answer are when you need to make a particular point with subtlety, without offending someone directly or they need to be put politely in their place! Remember also that the message is inferred by the recipient; if they don't like it you can always remind them that actually you did not say anything.

Remember that silence
is sometimes
the best answer

133

Setbacks or failure: get over it, move on

Instead of us seeing setbacks as a test of our resolve, many people get bogged down in frustration and reflection. As we saw with the quotation "when in a hole, stop digging" one should not flog a dead horse but neither should one waste time brooding over mistakes or failures. Recognise that there will be these times. Accept them, learn, correct them if you can and above all move on. Move on in a task sense but above all in an emotional sense.

Learning to let go of the past is the enabler to reaching out and grasping the future. In ocean yacht racing, many crews have used the phrase "leave it on the next wave." This means don't waste time arguing, moaning or wishing you had done something else – get on with the future as the past is gone. You can't turn the clock back.

I have met a number of people who get emotionally hijacked by setbacks. Their emotions are heightened and over-filled by negative emotions that linger far too long. This is destabilising and prevents future success. It really is important to get over setbacks – not doing so harms health. Conversely resilient people rarely give in to being hijacked in this way. They accept failures and learn. Self-awareness has immense value, especially in the workplace.

Another aspect of people who have difficulty getting over such problems is the obsessive type who cannot let go. "Winning isn't everything....it's the <u>only</u> thing" illustrates the kind of obsessive approach that dilutes perspective – the ability to step back and learn.

Setbacks or failure:
get over it, move on

If your stressful life requires ever more expensive recreation, do something low cost with zero expectation – then you can't be disappointed

Many of my friends have followed leisure pursuits where each successive holiday or hobby event requires ever more expensive forms of satisfaction. This is an addictive tendency: the harder you work the more you need luxurious holidays. The more luxurious they become the more money you need so you have to work even harder.

When chartering boats I started on a 28 foot vessel but progressed to a 36 then a 46 then a 53 then a 60 then a 65. At that point, I realised just how expensive it had become and that the law of diminishing returns had set in with a vengeance.

Every so often, everyone should do something as cheaply as possible. By having zero expectation, you really cannot be disappointed. The strange thing is that one values very different aspects: the friendliness of the people, the scenery, the simple life, colours and light. This can be a great source of stress relief. Compare that to the person who went wild because the cup delivered by the five star room service had a small crack in it!

The more we gamble on the expectation of having a great time, the more risky it becomes. And the more we gamble, the more disappointing and the greater the loss when things don't live up to our ever higher expectations.

The problem is that once a few things start to look wrong, our minds go looking for more when the stakes are too high. Our tolerance levels diminish and the value of the experience is lost.

If your stressful life requires
ever more expensive recreation,
do something low cost
with zero expectation
– then you can't be disappointed

There are those who happen to the world and those for whom the world happens to them

I know it is dangerous to over-simplify but in the final analysis, I do believe there are two types of person: those who make an impact, who take the initiative and who are not satisfied with mediocrity as opposed to those who drift, go with the flow and do not innovate. I am not suggesting that one type of person is more valuable or valued than the other. It is always a mixed blessing: those who happen to the world frequently experience more frustration whereas those for whom the world happens to them can sometimes be more "laid back" and more satisfied.

Those who happen to the world make an impact constructively, they influence with integrity, and they are remembered. Frequently it is their refusal to accept sub-standard service, products, situations and so on, that drives them to take action. As a result, their experience of life is enriched – by both good and bad experiences. Learning from these is all part of acquiring inner strength.

Perhaps the greatest value of "happening to the world" is the enriched experience and where it can take you. Most of us can give examples of people who through networking or taking the initiative have benefited. Whether it is knowing how to complain constructively, or helping someone who reciprocates or simply developing new friendships, the value is clear. But don't think all contact will lead to constructive experience. Instead recognise that life is a journey in all its richness. There are good experiences and there are learning experiences – actually very few indeed are "bad."

There are those
who happen to the world
and those for whom
the world happens to them

Leadership includes both strength and humility

The great leaders invite people to follow them on a journey. In turn, they willingly follow – there is no compulsion. The weaker leaders need some form of coercion or threat. Those who are even weaker, lead through fear.

The humility of great leaders shows them to be human, they listen and take advice. They are realists and pragmatists and they learn from their mistakes. They are not egotistical.

Think about all the great people you have admired through your life. What were or are their defining characteristics? What are the common themes? I suspect strength, judgement, consistency, integrity and your respect for them may feature on your list. We follow because we believe the leader is acting in our best interests. Hardly surprising that the Sandhurst motto is "To serve to lead."

Now consider the common themes relating to resilient people you know: is there any overlap? I suspect there may be. Those with such strength often have leadership capabilities. It was once said that members of the British Army's elite SAS division were some of the most humble leaders you could meet. Their team-work and mission execution however are legendary.

In a Wiki world of ubiquitous information, simply barking orders no longer works. So observe all leaders for their combination of both strength and humility. One without the other is not good. Consider also your impact on others if you are a leader or aspire to leadership.

Leadership includes both strength and humility

When you stumble, never crumble

Despite its poetic nature, this quotation contains valuable advice on keeping a level head, not losing your resolve or dignity and it is instructive on learning the lesson.

It is therefore a mine of advice. Let's face it, we all stumble from time to time. The enduring question is "how will you react, recover and learn from the experience?" Failure is nothing new. Neither is being less successful in a project than we would have liked. Learning the lesson and returning with renewed resolve or reaching a slightly different outcome via a different route are all perfectly valid. Remember, climbing Everest does not have to be done by the hardest route. There are easier routes. They may have been climbed before but if your goal is to stand on top of the world, the route is irrelevant: the outcome is what counts.

People who crumble waste everything: their time, effort, energy, emotional capital and of course the learning opportunity. In learning the lesson, ask yourself ten questions: What happened? How do I feel about that? Why do I feel that way? Why did it happen? Was it inevitable? Could I have done anything differently? What learning do I take from the experience? What was the underlying cause? What countermeasures can I put in place? How can things be different next time?

Accepting failure also contributes to the humility that is such an important characteristic of true leaders. The fact of stumbling shrinks into insignificance for those who learn the lesson. In fact those who subsequently get things right do so with greater strength, more visibility, greater recognition and more appreciation. People who win in adversity tend to be valued more highly than those who do so with ease.

When you stumble,
never crumble

Would you like to sit next to you at dinner?

This is a very helpful way of getting people to stand outside themselves and think about how they are seen, what is the shadow they cast, what their impact is and also how balanced their lives are.

It is a very useful learning device. It causes people to try and see themselves as others see them. With practice, this technique can be very illuminating. It can help you to understand whether you are boring someone; whether you are contributing too much or too little. If nothing else, it should prompt you to ask others for feedback and to inject questions and have check-points in your conversations.

It is strange how just a few questions to check the other person is still mentally engaged can elicit reciprocal conversation that leads to an enriched dialogue. Recognise that most people like talking about themselves. Give them the opportunity and see where that takes the conversation. Make linkages between your experiences.

The failing I have seen time and again is the person who is "locked on transmit." They are so keen to impress or to influence, that they appear incapable of reading some very simple signs that they have overstepped the mark. I was once party to a discussion on holiday home ownership. The novice enthusiast was obsessed and locked on transmit to their host about navigating the complexities of overseas house purchase. They were blind to the host's polite interjections. At the end of the evening, as they got into their car, they said to the host "you should think about doing it." The host replied, "I did – we bought 3 years ago and I could have told you all about it." Such was the lost opportunity.

Would you like to sit next
to you at dinner?

Fail to prepare means prepare to fail

There is a certain attraction of the mirror image in this quotation that makes it memorable and succinct. The advice however starts with an implicit appreciation of context. Without that, it would be difficult to know what and how to prepare. People with inner strength make a habit of trying to understand exactly what is required. I have encountered some people who think that asking contextual queries is a sign of weakness. Quite the reverse: seeking clarification and asking the right questions normally earns respect and helps others to ensure their requirements are clear. So start with the end in mind.

Preparation itself can be the subject of clarification too. "What would a successful presentation look like?" is a useful tool.

By understanding the key requirements one can then think about who the key stakeholders are. By understanding their needs you can improve your preparation – by answering their likely questions. At work, always consider stakeholder management: "Throw away the organisation chart – draw the influence chart." I think this can apply as much to life outside work as it does to the business environment.

By allowing enough time to prepare and also allowing time for last minute adjustment, you can be far more relaxed, calm and ready to shine. We shall explore some aspects of time management later but always always set time boundaries. That way you can prepare appropriately. If you don't, then stand by for missing the mark – or at best not getting it quite right. As they say: fail to prepare = prepare to fail.

Fail to prepare means
prepare to fail

Winners think correctly under pressure

One hallmark of champions is their ability, consistently, to think correctly under pressure. In the Olympic year of 2012 I had the privilege of meeting Sir Clive Woodward – coach for Team GB that achieved the best performance in 100 years. He explained how even a small amount of scenario planning helped give a competitive edge. He told a story of how at an Olympic final, a demonstration and intruder disrupted the diving final. The favourites were so shocked and distracted by this, they made mistakes that cost them the gold medal. The surprise winners came from nowhere. This was because they had mentally rehearsed what would happen if an alarm went off just as they were about to dive. They had also considered what they might do in the event of a fire, an evacuation, a blackout and so on. The act of rehearsing these things in one's mind – even only in outline, can lead to better decisions under pressure.

They say your chances of escaping from an aircraft emergency are much enhanced if you know exactly how many seat rows forward and behind you are the nearest exits. Seconds save lives in smoke filled dark aircraft cabins. So the next time you settle into your seat, ask your friendly co-passenger to close their eyes and name the number of row forward and aft to the nearest exit. In more than 30 years of my own flying, no one has ever been able to answer this question – despite the cabin crew announcing "Please take time to note where your nearest exit is, recognising that the nearest one may be behind you."

I am not advocating paranoia. I am simply saying, let's think about what might happen when we are under pressure. And that lifts some of the pressure, especially at work.

Winners think correctly
under pressure

Things work out best for those who make the best of the way things work out

There is a popular misconception that some people have all the luck and that things invariably work out better for them. The key to understanding this quotation is an appreciation of flexibility. Instead of lamenting a less than perfect situation, people with a flexible approach build on what they have and are prepared to alter their route to the solution.

There are people who recognise situations for what they are then apply flexible creativity and energy to optimise the situation. So the way things work out is augmented by a constructive approach – maybe it takes more energy, more effort and more resources but eventually making the most of what there is leads to a better outcome.

I am sure you can think of examples. If you fail your "A" levels, do you drop out or redouble your resolve to either re-take them or pursue a higher education course other than a traditional university degree? People who have the bridge removed in front of them but who can see stepping-stones can navigate their way forward. Those who fail to see the opportunity of stepping-stones tend towards paralysis. At work, nothing really goes completely to plan. But having a "Plan B" plus an agile approach enables continual steering onto the target.

The path of continual optimisation, of variation and taking the bends in the metaphorical road actually keep you on track. The track may be longer than planned but it is still the track. Preparation is also helpful as is expecting change and things not going to plan. The co-incidence of effective preparation with unexpected opportunity is very valuable indeed. That's when magic happens.

Things work out best
for those who make the best
of the way things work out

Time flies; be the pilot

The popular view is that work expands to fill the time available. But it is more complicated than that. Time management is about setting priorities and absolutes. It is also about courage: the courage to say "no" when asked to attend a meeting at a ridiculous time. This is the same courage to reject a meeting, shopping trip or social call if you know it to be wasteful of your most precious resource – your time.

So take control. Recognise that there will always be more to do, so set your limits. People with inner strength set their time priorities and do not allow others to infringe their rights in terms of time. They take steps to reduce and contain the attempts of others to waste their time. They are not stressed by constant interruptions or the need to respond instantly. Instead they set appropriate time aside and they know their limits. They can politely say "no" to a request to do more. They frequently do so by saying "you have already asked me to do these various things. My capacity is full. So if I do this new thing, which of the previous list is coming off the list?" It takes bravery the first time you say this but it gets easier the more you do it. The worst thing is to say "yes" to something when you know the answer is "no" – because there simply isn't the time.

So climb into that pilot's seat at the front of time. Strap yourself in – you are the pilot. You choose, you are in control. You reject hijackers; they are screened out of your plane. Don't look back over lost time. Instead recognise the value of the future. You cannot turn the clock back but you can be the pilot of your current and future use of time

Time flies; be the pilot

North African proverb says it is easier to ride a camel in the direction it is going

We all know that for every proverb or quotation, there is another advising the very opposite point of view. The quotation on this page appears to fly in the face of much of this book. It appears to advocate compliance, acceptance, not challenging the status quo and simply "going with the flow."

However, the value of these quotations lies in the thought processes we go through when thinking about them. In this case, think about other cultures – what is their point of view? Why might another culture see things differently? Now consider why someone might find it easier to "go with the flow" rather than contest the status quo. The enlightenment that follows helps us to understand how best to operate within a system of rules and how to influence within an environment of constraint. We may not like the direction the camel is taking but with some effort, we can steer it – even if we cannot turn it around. Given that the camel has a mind of its own, we should also prepare ourselves for not being totally in control of something we normally might have control over (such as when driving a car for example.)

I like this quotation because it is multi-dimensional: other cultures, the definition of rationality, influence rather than arrogance, subtlety, operating within a system rather than outside it – with all the inherent risks. Add to that the unpredictability of the camel's mind and you will understand that one may not be able to isolate cause and effect.

Appreciating rational, irrational, emotional, political and then pragmatic attributes of any situation brings strength.

North African proverb says
it is easier to ride a camel
in the direction it is going

If you never change your mind, why have one?

It takes courage and strength to change your mind and admit it. For those who don't have enough, they experience frustration and stress because they have difficulty coming to terms with changing their stated position on something. For those who do have the courage, it is easier to admit they were wrong or badly informed – and to move on.

This is a sign of strength – to acknowledge being better informed or to have better understanding. The spin-off is that this strength enables people to admit to their mistakes and to move on far more easily than those who indulge in defensive behaviour.

This quotation therefore challenges us to review our thinking, to check we are properly briefed and remain up to date. The ability to re-evaluate, re-prioritise and exercise judgement are increasingly valued in today's faster world with ever more information available. Those who doggedly cling to outdated ideas face a bigger turning point if they have over-invested their emotional capital in their (now) outmoded belief.

At my school, pop group fan clubs were all the rage until one's chosen band went out of favour! Then last week's heroes suddenly became passé and a joke. Their followers were suddenly lesser people through the fickleness of fashion.

When you are utterly convinced of something, take time to reflect and ask yourself "Am I still sure?" Having the strength to review things reinforces a sense of balance and perspective. Having the strength to change your mind strangely adds yet more strength.

If you never change your mind,
why have one?

Education is what is left when you have forgotten everything you have been taught

Is education just everything you have been taught? I don't think so. My view is that education is no more than the operating system that one's intellectual processes work within. And just as a computer needs continual upgrades to its operating system, so we need life-long learning.

The educational input however is but a small sub-set of education overall. Hence this quotation: education is what is left after all the detailed input has been forgotten. It is what enables the enquiring mind to acquire and use knowledge; to form judgements, make decisions and act on information.

But you knew that already. Real perception understands the difference between the value of knowledge for its own sake and the value of applying it in social, economic and other contexts. Let's face it, most of us have met people who are undoubted experts but who are either totally unemployable or who have no social skills whatsoever.

I have met some very wise people who were illiterate and others who were boffins but could not get served at a bar. The application of education is what counts. People with inner strength know their unique qualities and their limitations. They work around these and put their capabilities to best use – sometimes using contacts and enlisting help where required. Remember Einstein once asked why he should learn some point of detail when he knew he could look it up in a book.

Finally, remember that knowing facts does not equal education. There is much more to it than that.

Education is what is left
when you have forgotten
everything you
have been taught

Life is a bed of roses, thorns and all

Taking the rough with the smooth is part of modern life. Only these days there is faster change, more unpredictable change and more extreme change. Or so we may think. But looking back in history there were far more fatalities through poverty, disease, accidents and starvation. Poverty is of course relative and whereas it used to be characterised by the absence of inside washing facilities, now it is having no home broadband network and web-enabled LED flat screen TV. I think the real challenge is moderating our perception of the rough/smooth when pressures from dual careers can drive stress into families. Perhaps the evolving definition of "quality of life" helps us to understand the changing concept of "thorns and all."

Beware appearances. Taken literally, a bunch of roses is one of the most appealing sights. However the stems, leaves and flowers conceal the thorns that can rip your skin. When presented with an image or impression, whether at work or outside of work, think about what hidden thorns there might be. Remember the easy life rarely came easily. I was once at a lunch party where the hosts appeared to be paragons of calm relaxation. On leaving, I asked whether they would be relaxing into the late afternoon. "Oh no" came the reply, we have 6 hours of email, conference calls and reporting to do. And that was on a Sunday.

If you think there are too many thorns, try to reset the balance to get more flowers! Remember everything has a cost and if the small luxuries you desire mean working 24 hours a day, perhaps the price is simply too high. Accept that, move on and moderate your requirement – if it is not worth it, it's not worth it.

Life is a bed of roses,
thorns and all

The impossible is impossible. Unless that is, you have the kind of money that says it isn't

The moral of this story is: make sure you know what you are getting yourself into. If someone asks you to do the impossible – don't accept it. If you get into an impossible situation, don't fool yourself that extracting yourself from it or resolving it are easy if they aren't. This is about pragmatism and realism. Once you have recognised a situation for what it really is, doing the impossible may actually require immeasurable resources. So don't go there in the first place.

I have found this quotation to be helpful when advising people and helping them acquire what I call hindsight from the future. Frequently people underestimate situations they could get into. For example if in a work situation an employer has breached someone's contract and the person is absolutely determined to have their day in court – it helps to review the situation pragmatically in the context of this quote.

Similarly, if someone's aspiration is completely unrealistic, help them to understand the meaning of this quotation. They may realise the price they need to pay is simply too large. Beware also those people who glibly say everything is easy without actually spelling out how and why. It is a common trait of inexperienced leaders who say "go on it's easy" when nothing could be further from the truth.

The overall coaching here is that extreme situations usually require even more extreme solutions to change them. By recognising situations for what they could become, we avoid getting into areas where huge resources are required to get back to normality. Armed with that sort of foresight builds resilience and strength.

The impossible __is__ impossible.
Unless that is,
you have the kind of money
that says it isn't

If you think universities are expensive, try ignorance

This was a car sticker on the back of a Morris traveller – a car that was already 40 years old when I saw it. The sentiment has immediate appeal by causing people to weigh the balance of costs: investment versus the cost of errors.

There is another perspective however: what is the risk you run by having people (or even yourself) insufficiently informed, or prepared for something. Ignorance has a far bigger cost but few people recognise it at the time.

How may times have you bought something and launched straight into it without reading the instruction manual? Of course few of us read it before unwrapping the product. As a child, I recall my father once trying to lever-off the top of a new dishwasher before realising it was a front opener.

Another perspective on this quotation is about perceptions of miss-spent youth. No matter how irritating students can be to the rest of the population, they do ultimately contribute to society in a very big way. So the price of perceived escape from the real world (drinking, socialising until the small hours, doing as little as possible, making a nuisance) is worth paying if ultimately society benefits from an educated population.

What is the all-up cost of education? It is hard to quantify just as the hidden cost of ignorance is even harder to quantify: stress, damage rectification, inefficiency, sub-optimal decisions and waste to name a few. Being able to judge the balance between the resources needed for investment versus the risk of not having it, is a valuable skill.

If you think universities
are expensive,
try ignorance

Which perspective: Fog in channel, continent cut off?

Context is everything. It never ceases to amaze me how groups take an introspective view of their world. Theirs is the reference standard against which everything is judged. We assume that our society is the best and our way of doing things is the best. We all say the BBC is the one true and trustworthy broadcaster – but we have explored some interesting experience of syndicated news video earlier. In the UK we assume our healthcare is (or was) the very best. Any yet our life expectancy is really no different to that of the other advanced European economies.

But the danger of parochialism is that it leads to assumptions that are so obviously wrong to others – but some people just can't see this. My European friends tend to see the UK as the Haverford West of Europe: stuck out at the most western extreme, out of the mainstream and away from the action. While we might think the continent has been cut off by fog, it never occurs to us that the continent may not care about what lies out there in the fog. I exaggerate to make the point but having a wider perspective helps to moderate the inward looking perceptions so many people have.

Someone in Macau asked me where I was from. "London" I replied. They looked quizzically and asked "Why should I be interested in a small island off the far coast of Europe?" At another time, I told some friends I was working in Belo Horizonte, Brazil. They thought "small village?" I said "Yes, a small town of 4.5m people."

Always consider the view from the opposite end of the telescope, then ask yourself "Am I looking through the right end in the first place?"

Which perspective:
Fog in channel,
continent cut off?

The immediate neighbours of tolerance are indifference and apathy

"Live and let live" I hear you say. But how much and how far? How far should we accept things that go against our ethics and culture? By thinking about the "envelope" of what is acceptable, we constantly define behaviour and the rules of social responsibility.

While we might tolerate someone dropping litter in the street we all feel a greater sense of indignation at "fly-tipping" ie: the blatant dumping of rubbish - usually industrial or building waste in our streets.

Tolerance is fine and is normally to be encouraged but knowing how to recognise apathy is also important. People with inner strength do not go along with the silent majority. They speak up and they speak out where there is clear injustice or abuse of rules, moral codes or other social mores. They are not surrogate policemen; they simply know what they stand for and have the confidence to articulate it. At work, everyone knows who the passengers are. Credit is always given to managers who have the strength to deal with such situations. It may take bravery but if you can't change the people – you have to change the people.

Sadly history is littered with well meaning individuals who tolerated minor misdemeanours without seeing the bigger picture – the thin end of the wedge. By the time they had come to appreciate the erosion of liberty it was too late, and for example, a totalitarian government had been elected.

By understanding the limits of reasonableness, people stay engaged with family, community and society.

The immediate neighbours of tolerance are indifference and apathy

The time to deal with a problem is before
it becomes a bigger one

Procrastination and avoidance are very common characteristics. I think this illustrates human nature that seeks pleasure and avoids pain. Many people however mistakenly believe that pain can be avoided by simply ignoring the issue. Clearly there are some problems that will resolve themselves: they will time-expire, the issue will be forgotten or it will simply "blow over." Yet the important problems tend not to fall into these categories. Financial, physical, relationship and many other areas tend to get worse not better with time.

It takes bravery to confront a problem. But once one starts getting used to the challenge – and one knows that delay would mean a bigger challenge, things do get easier: one's confidence and strength to confront the issue improve.

Whenever I have been asked for advice on when and how to deal with problems, I have used this quotation. People consistently report back that it is good advice. They don't like it but having intervened they frequently uncover other issues which had been hidden. By addressing the totality of the problem they realise things could have got much worse.

It is better to sell your investment when you have lost 25% rather than lose 50% or more. Also, by adopting an action mentality and by taking action, you train yourself to confront issues and to deal with them. This helps people to spot problems earlier and take corrective action sooner and sooner. And hey presto! This means they gradually face fewer problems. And that in turn reduces stress and increases strength.

The time to deal
with a problem
is before it becomes
a bigger one

German proverb says: He who speaks the truth needs a fast horse

If you need to speak the blunt truth, make sure you have a means of exit. This could mean a physical exit (ie saddling up your horse and getting out of town) or it could mean a diplomatic exit ie: using diplomacy to prevent you personally being associated with the message. Or perhaps it could mean an emotional exit. If you are associated with the message, could you distance yourself from it or at least do some damage limitation?

All this supposes that you need to speak in a high risk and challenging way. There are circumstances where this may be necessary. My observation is that ethical dilemmas are the most frequent. Let us suppose you find it impossible to continue with something because "the Emperor has no clothes" and you are the only one who can see it.

You could simply assert that the Emperor has no clothes and therefore you renounce all association or you resign or you absent yourself. That is the end of your relationship. Alternatively you could frame the message in terms more acceptable, such as by asking others a series of questions whereby their own analysis leads them to the correct conclusion. As a further alternative you could make the point, refer to the clear evidence, cite other examples and any other independent corroboration. You could then make an immediate offer of assistance to help address the problem and resolve the issue.

For me the value of this quotation is that it causes people to think through how their speaking will be received. If the message really is very high risk, make sure you at least have a horse saddled and ready!

German proverb says:
He who speaks the truth needs
a fast horse

Judge your successes by what you had to give up in order to get them

I really like this one because so many people appear to have a fixation with materialism, they acquire unimaginable skill in ignoring its cost. And I am not just talking about money.

A former colleague was elevated to an airline frequent flyers' club top tier. He was so proud to have the gold card. I asked about the cost – he didn't understand. When I mentioned all the time spent away from family and baggage labels effectively saying "steal me: expensive computer inside" he still didn't get the point. Sadly his marriage failed four years later.

So there is usually a trade-off to be done. I have long held the view that most people can ultimately have whatever they want. It is simply a question of what they are prepared to give up in order to achieve it. This is close to the notion of knowing when to stop and the law of diminishing returns. Working twice as hard for a high fashion product poses the question "is it worth it?" – if the (allegedly) lesser product has full functionality.

By all means aim for the stars. Set audacious ambitions. But be aware of what will be required to achieve them. This awareness will equip you to address the unexpected challenges that occur. The good life rarely comes easily. A student friend of mine once worked on a building site all summer to save for a car. When he finally bought it he felt he had earned every single nut, bolt and screw of it. And it nearly cost him his life.

The real secret though is achieving any success that costs very little. That builds resilience and strength.

Judge your successes
by what you had to give up
in order to get them

Dutch proverb says: You can't boil soup
if you keep adding cold water

Anyone old enough to remember defence projects in the 1960s will recall the TSR2. This was a fighter/bomber aircraft project. It became a classic business school case study on how not to run projects. The lack of clarity, accountability and governance meant it suffered from "scope creep." Apparently, the military kept changing the specification and slowly but surely said "If we could just make it go this little bit faster, with this slightly extended range….." And then of course it needed more powerful engines and then a stronger airframe. Eventually the costs were deemed too high and the project was scrapped.

While this was a case of people constantly pouring in cold water, we should consider situations where cold water comes into the project through nobody's fault but it is still unstoppable. Having some capability in reserve and of course a "Plan B" and "C" are good precautions.

We all know the phrase about the last straw breaking the camel's back. Yet many people cannot see the damage done by distraction, scope creep, and additional but unrelated tasks. So if you want to write a book about inner strength, it can't be done if professional life, family, gardening requirements, home DIY, work commitments and other requirements overwhelm it.

At work, we all know that SMART objectives are a good way of keeping focused. But do we take enough time to agree the essential few objectives that must be done? I once tried to impress a new boss by telling him everything I was handling. He said "Good; but from now on I want you to do just this one and that one. Nothing else."

Dutch proverb says:
You can't boil soup
if you keep adding
cold water

Trust the judgement of your wife/husband. If she/he had the good sense to marry you there must be further good sense for you to benefit from

It is very easy for couples to drift into two parallel but separate lives, particularly when both are busy professionals. We tend to see each other in context. And sometimes those contexts rarely coincide. By sharing information, hopes and fears one can benefit from advice in surprising ways. Frequently a new perspective can open a whole new line of thinking and opportunity.

The value of input from your spouse is that she/he will be able to see you as others see you. This external perspective always adds a new dimension. The old cliché is that a problem shared is a problem halved. However that ignores the more constructive perspective about opportunities discussed, dilemmas resolved and opportunities multiplied.

Even simple questions such as "what about holidays this year – high cost, high expectation or low cost, no expectation?" can produce a very rich discussion.

The real purpose of this quotation though is to get people talking about meaningful things. A survey in the early years of the 21st century revealed that most married couples spent just 17 minutes in meaningful conversation each day. The rest of their time was fully occupied with routine predictability. And still people deny they are leading parallel lives! So trust the judgement of your spouse – their wisdom may surprise you. "What do you think? is a surprisingly powerful question.

Trust the judgement
of your wife/husband.
If she/he had the good sense
to marry you there must be
further good sense
for you to benefit from

Learn the law of diminishing returns. A £20 bottle of wine may be twice as good as a £10 bottle but twice as good again is £80 then £500

I think all manufacturers and suppliers of goods and services these days use marketing to segment product ranges. They then apply pricing structures to increase margins at the high end of the range. From there it is only a simple sales technique to persuade people to move up the range. This also applies to brands. Once you have established a premium brand, you charge as much as the market will bear. When did the price you pay for something every bear any relationship to the fundamental raw material cost? Never.

So whether we are talking about cosmetics, TV screens, hotels, ladies handbags, home cinema equipment, cars, or even private jets, beware the law of diminishing returns.

Ask yourself how far you are prepared to go to move up the range? I once even saw an advertisement for three stereos from the same manufacturer with the subtitle: "Good"... "Better"... "Best." And surprise surprise the margins doubled each time. As a child I wondered why my father's cars were usually the gadget-free base model. On reflection I think this was wise: buying a better engineered model rather than a cheap one with all the extras was probably the wiser decision.

So the next time you ponder the enjoyment of a bottle of wine, think about how much additional refreshment and enjoyment a doubling and quadrupling of price will bring as you work your way up the range. How far will you go and why? Of course go as far as you like....but have the strength to know why you are doing it. Oh, and do pass the Petrus along the table!

Learn the law
of diminishing returns.
A £20 bottle of wine may be
twice as good as a £10 bottle
but twice as good again
is £80 then £500

Don't think the easy life comes easily.
Getting what you want demands hard work,
application and persistence.
The real skill is knowing how far to go.

Outer appearances can of course deceive. However, some people think beyond the immediate presentation of others. What may appear to be the easily life almost invariably comes through much harder work and dedication then we can ever imagine. We gloss over the challenges – but if it really was that easy, why don't you see it more often? If something looks or sounds too good to be true – it probably is.

Assuming you are prepared to do what is required to achieve a particular goal, hard work, focus and persistence are all needed. It is rarely easy and if others think you simply had good luck then it is your decision whether you allow that perception to persist. We have already talked about the laid-back lunch party hosts who were going to work all Sunday afternoon and evening to stay on top of their business commitments.

Some people try to create an impression of living the easy life, which just might signify some deep insecurity. As a child, I was fortunate to grow up in a substantial 6 bedroom Victorian house. When my parents came to sell it, the estate agent said "don't judge a sausage by its skin." I found out much later that this referred to a couple who arrived in a luxury supercar to view the house. The viewing was detailed, serious and implied a generous offer would be forthcoming. The agent later apologised having discovered that the vehicle was hired, many viewings had taken place but the couple had not made a single offer anywhere.

Don't think the easy life
comes easily.
Getting what you want
demands hard work,
application and persistence.
The real skill is knowing
how far to go.

You can't turn back the clock

This succinct quotation can be a valuable source of guidance in so many situations. It can refer to the ageing process: the "if only" lament; the absence of forward-looking enthusiasm and so many other things.

Whenever we are in a difficult situation, we tend to think about what might have happened if things had turned out differently. People with inner strength experience this far less than the majority of the population simply because they have thought through things and planned better. Also, rather than look back sentimentally, they understand that the future is more important and they have the strength and courage to address it.

Recognising that "we are where we are" is usually the first step to facing the future and addressing what needs to be done. This can be very liberating because it helps people to let go of the past – the past that is holding them back, paralysing the steps to improvement, a solution or attainment of a goal. I am not trying to deny the value of the past. I am simply saying that using it to inform the future rather than prevent it, brings more value.

Knowing that one can't turn back the clock helps us in a number of ways: first it can create a renewed sense of urgency. Secondly it prompts people to make choices where perhaps previously they had been avoided. Thirdly, it helps people to stop worrying about how and why they are where they are. Fourthly it encourages people to focus on the future and on improvement/resolution. Fifthly, it brings the need for action into sharper relief. Finally, one point about punctuality: you can beat the clock. The best way to avoid missing the train is to get to the platform early!

You can't turn back the clock

Sometimes good taste and ambition can be a curse. You see so much that is not right

It was once said that "America doesn't claim to have good taste…it just tastes good." For those who appreciate the difference between good and bad design, having that knowledge can create a personal tension. After all, ignorance is bliss. Nevertheless, our understanding of perfection should not cause us to despise reality, which is frequently less than perfect.

Someone once said to me that many conscientious people don't realise how good they are. They assume that everyone else it at least as good if not better. This is because their frame of reference is their own capability. In addition, those things that come easily to them are assumed to be easy for others. The reality of course is that many others may marvel at how the first person can do what they do – and with such apparent ease and composure.

Those with ambition tend to be driven, compelled to do more and do better. They are not complacent: "enough" is not good enough. So they face frustration when surrounded by those with less drive and impatience. For me, the ability to recognise why people are driven – what is the grit in their oyster is extremely valuable. Once that is understood, their motivation makes better sense. Also, understanding what drives people helps one to predict their ultimate likelihood of achieving their objectives – and maybe your own.

So don't be too frustrated by mediocrity. Try to create an advantage where you have seen something that others have not. Then try and make ambition infectious. It can work wonders at work.

Sometimes good taste and
ambition can be a curse.
You see so much
that is not right

When in a dilemma step back and tell yourself to:
Do the right thing

Seeing the wood for the trees is a common issue facing people who are stressed with complex – or seemingly complex problems. Dilemmas and particularly ethical dilemmas are even more difficult. The ability to stand back and "unpack" the issue into smaller elements is essential to get to the best possible outcome. We know this and yet it becomes very difficult to advise ourselves.

One solution is to talk things through with someone. Remaining impartial when it's personal is never easy. However my observation is that a clear sense of ethics and a strong set of values are the best compass. Being guided by these values helps to cut through to the core issues. Key to this is the ability to distance oneself and to step back from the situation. We could have a "head versus heart" debate here but even the slightest amount of impartiality is very helpful. In a world of financial and banking scandals, the so-called "Daily Mail" test is instructive. If you are thinking about a solution or course of action, how would you feel if it was reported in the tabloid press?

There can never be an easy answer for all the complexity of modern life but I am reminded of an early lesson in my career: The story is of the junior Human Resources professional who is given a huge book that reportedly has all the business answers. He examines the front and opens the vast leather bound cover hoping to see tens of thousands of words. Instead there are only four. All the pages beyond the first page are blank.

The first page simply said: "Do the right thing."

When in a dilemma
step back and tell yourself to:
Do the right thing

Diplomacy is telling someone to go to Hell such that they look forward to the journey

There is a certain humour about this quotation. Yet the advice it gives is instructive: the message is less important than the action or behavioural change that follows. Learning the skill to criticise so that the recipient accepts it, internalises it and changes behaviour without reproach is a very valuable skill.

In part, the ABC (appreciation before criticism) rule helps. Also, focusing on the behaviour rather than the person helps. Use of the word "and" instead of "but" can be extremely helpful. Finally, creating a compelling desire for change or helping people to understand the prize can all help you gain people's trust. In this way they are more likely to look forward to the journey – whatever the destination.

Some people have misunderstood the motivation behind this quotation. They think it is about tricking or cheating people – they look forward to the journey because they do not appreciate that it leads to Hell. That is low integrity behaviour. Diplomacy is about framing an instructive message in a way that it is understood, accepted and acted upon in the full knowledge that the main thrust of the message is challenging and critical.

But put carefully, who wouldn't want to improve? Provided there is no loss of face, most people would want to prove the critics wrong. So success is about communicating a motivational message rather than one provoking revenge. Perhaps all communication should have the response in mind: what do you want people to think, feel and do as a result?

Diplomacy is telling someone
to go to Hell such that they
look forward to the journey

The best way to predict the future is to create it

A very good piece of advice once given to me was "write the minutes of the meeting before the meeting." This was not aimed at unfair influence or an attempt at stifling debate. It was a guide to direct one's thinking, chairmanship and to ensure that the proper issues were addressed and outcomes decided upon.

Creation is better than forecasting or predicting. Working on the principle that it is better to act your way into a new way of thinking….it is action that takes tangible steps towards the future. While writing this book, my mother said she needed to get back to writing her autobiography. She had been talking about writing this for about 20 years but had only succeeded in typing 5 or 6 pages. I said I didn't believe she would ever get any further because the motivation and drive simply weren't there. Procrastination and explanations were offered – all perfectly plausible however there was no result. Had she set a plan to write a page a day or even a line a day, twenty years would have produced the finished result.

So one step at a time – people who are focused and determined make progress. However slow, as long as one keeps up the march, one will get there. Or as the Chinese say: a journey of a thousand miles begins with a single step.

The motivational aspect of making progress - however slow, helps to build confidence and velocity. Getting to the first fifty pages in this book was real progress. The next fifty were much easier and now as I near two hundred, the goal is almost on the horizon. It is very strengthening to know you are getting there.

The best way
to predict the future
is to create it

Get out of your own way

This quotation is similar to the notion of "argue for your limitations and they are surely yours." I have had various conversations with people over the years where their assumption was that something cannot be done. Having convinced themselves that it is impossible, they shrug their shoulders and move on to something else.

One of my own "ah-ha" moments came from a conversation with my father many years ago. I had enjoyed an exceptional bottle of Alsace wine and lamented its unavailability in the UK. He simply said "You have the producer's name on the label, why not write to them? Surely you aren't going to be defeated by such a simple thing?" Bear in mind that this was more than ten years before the internet and Google. But his advice led to a very interesting sequence of events: I wrote to the producer who replied saying they would be exhibiting in London at a trade fair in the City in 6 weeks time. They asked me which wines I would like them to bring over and whether I would like a free pass into the trade fair. Six weeks later I was enjoying a tasting with the producer, learning about the terroir, climate and production methods. They had brought over six cases especially for me and I paid them the appropriate price. It was not until I had the wines safely back at home that I realised having paid in French Francs, we had forgotten about any UK tax. Several years later the product was available in the UK via a retail warehouse – at three times the price of course.

This may appear a trite example but it illustrates that the pursuit of one's goal can lead to some unexpectedly good results.

Get out of your own way

Drive like Hell and you'll soon be there

The problem is - most people think this one is about motoring. I see it as much more far reaching than that. Naturally, there is the image of driving like a maniac which exposes you to unacceptable risks and almost certain death.

But there is a more subtle interpretation too: those who live life in a reckless manner, without any concern for their impact on others will sooner or later find out that they have few friends and no close relationships. By "driving like Hell" they have devoted all their emotional energy and time to a single-track pursuit. This might be making as much money as possible ("and to hell with the consequences"), career ("and who cares who I step on as I climb the greasy pole") or the acquisition of knowledge/skill ("and nothing else matters.") By having a complete imbalance in their lives these people fail to recognise the warning signals that there is actually nothing else in their lives.

Please bear in mind that the faster you drive, the sooner you are likely to reach a possibly unexpected destination. There will always be times of exception. I once worked nearly 100 hours in a week. But if you overdraw on the psychological bank account of relationships, you need to repay the debt. Investing in relationships builds wealth beyond money.

Think also about how one is seen by others. The faster people are perceived to be "driving" the more others may disengage with them. The lost opportunity could be large. After all, one of the benefits of networking is the help available from others. And an effective network accelerates productivity.

Drive like Hell
and you'll soon be there

Those who can't laugh at themselves
leave the job to others

This follows on from the previous quotation. If you are so intense that you cannot step back or cannot make time for others, the chances are you will be suffering from a humour deficit. Think about the humorous side of everything. Humour reduces stress, aids creativity and promotes health. If you can't laugh about yourself from time to time – you really will leave the job to others. They will see the folly of your endeavours or attitude or your general demeanour. Laughter facilitates engagement with others. It also helps us to see a much broader picture. The value of that is the improvement to decision making. If as a result of seeing the funny side of something you make a more informed decision – it signals fewer mistakes, less re-work, less "situation recovery" and so on.

As children, my brother and I were once reprimanded for failing to take sufficient care when using a fork to put pickled beetroot on our plates from a serving dish. The family best tablecloth was underneath. My father insisted on demonstrating best practice – only the beetroot fell off his fork back into the dish – splashing beetroot colour vinegar all over the cloth. He could have become angry or insisted on the merits of his attempt. But having paused for a few seconds we all laughed hysterically and learned the lesson. The story was still re-told more than 40 years after it happened. The instructional message was all the more powerful by virtue of the humour. And the mistake never happened again.

Those who can't laugh at
themselves
leave the job to others

Be the change you want to see in the world

It is no use complaining about everyone and everything else if one cannot act as a role model for the conduct and ethics one wants to see. Set an example – remember the people who happen to the world. The world does not just happen to them. They are in control and are influential both in a direct way and indirectly: subtly, in ways that impact others. They cast a shadow that is constructive and positive. A word of caution: at work, some people don't realise that the more senior they get, the bigger the shadow they cast. At the top, their every move, word, action and behaviour are watched and noted.

By setting an example one is developing and projecting one's own "brand" – what one stands for. It also helps to distinguish the stronger people from those who are simply followers of fashion. It is also part of being a first class version of yourself rather than a second class imitation of someone else.

If I think of the influential people who have made a profound impression on me, I think of those who have a strong sense of their personal values, they behave with integrity and they are consistent. Mentors typically have a reputation for wisdom, balance and knowledge – but also integrity.

Ask yourself whether you are seen as a mentor or guiding influence. If not, what needs to change in order for this to be true? I think that having a strong personal brand will help. Respect is earned by people who are abundantly clear what they stand for and whose ethics and integrity are never in doubt.

Be the change
you want to see in the world

Keep your eyes focused on what cannot be seen

By now I expect you are wondering whether your author has taken leave of his senses. How can you possibly focus your eyes on something invisible? But there lies the depth of this quotation. It is an invitation to concentrate not just on the immediate agenda – but on the hidden agenda. It can take a lot of looking before you learn to see.

I am reminded of an airline TV advertisement. Everywhere the internet is used for sales proposals to be sent by email. One bidder appreciates the importance of personal relationships and flies to visit the prospective customer. After the second face-to-face visit, this supplier wins the deal. The loser was convinced of the merit of his proposal but had failed to see the bigger picture. He had not kept focused on what could not be seen: the trust relationship.

Please don't rely on facts alone. For sure they are important but they are not the whole picture.

This quotation is about thinking ahead and thinking round the next few corners. It is also about recognising situations for what they could turn into and paying special attention to them. It is also about focusing on what might appear obvious to you but which appears to be invisible to others – and vice versa.

I learned today of a schoolboy who bought the entire stock of nuts from his school shop because they were at their sell-by date. He bought them at half price. His fellow pupils did not understand why he had bought the whole supply but willingly bought them from him at a very reasonable 25% discount off the normal price. They did not realise the 50% profit margin made on each packet!

Keep your eyes focused
on what cannot be seen

Less is more

I suspect this common saying is not fully understood by everyone. Its principle is that unnecessary detail detracts from the essential message. Whether you are writing an essay, giving a speech, furnishing your home or writing a piece of music, un-necessary embellishment gets in the way of understanding.

I was once told that when giving a speech, always give a pause between each idea. There are two reasons for this: first, no one falls asleep in silence. Second, no one will remember a single word of what you said. Instead all they will remember is the internal debate they had with themselves while you delivered your speech. Apart from that, people frequently have difficulty remembering more than three main points anyway.

Bombarding people with millions of figures doesn't work. Neither does death by PowerPoint. Or as one colleague once said: "Martin Luther King didn't need slides."

When I think of all the very best design statements, they are those with clean lines and an elegant simplicity. When I think about the best interiors, they are simple and un-cluttered. When I think of the finest minds, they are clear, concise, insightful but above all simplistic. Such people can communicate complexity in disarmingly simple ways. My observation is that the more complex an answer the more likely it is that the speaker lacks confidence in their subject. We should discuss things in elegantly simple ways that remove complexity. The more people we want to influence, the simpler the message needs to be. This is especially important in work and leadership situations.

Less is more

Live simply; life is in the details: calling an old friend, making something, an early morning walk, observing things unseen by others

Complexity in life fuels stress. Competitive lives may be essential in the modern world but it should not be all-consuming. I once overheard the phrase "Winning isn't everything….it's the ONLY thing." Clearly the person was obsessed. I think that people who have the competitive parts of their lives under control do so (in part) by keeping the small simple things alive and on their agenda. That takes strength. Making time for people, doing something with low or no monetary value but very high personal value helps to maintain that essential balance. While days last hours, moments last a lifetime.

Perhaps we need to move away from consumption being the primary source of experience. On my train journeys to and from London I catch fleeting glimpses of wild rabbits. I am convinced no one else sees them as the train speeds past. It is surprising how much understanding one can accumulate about their social system, hierarchy, protective mechanisms regarding predators and their life cycle. For me, this helps preserve a sense of perspective in a frenetic world. There is also a certain satisfaction in knowing that few others have seen what I see.

Never underestimate the value of personal acts of good will. I once made a gold crown for my wife as a Christmas present. That may sound exotic and expensive. However it was made from cardboard, glue and aerosol gold paint. But its profile was copied from the crown of Aragon (from a crest on a Spanish taxi). For her, this had far more meaning than the other more expensive presents I bought.

Live simply; life is in the details:
calling an old friend,
making something,
an early morning walk,
observing things unseen
by others

Reframe the context

We have already examined the notion of the mind being its own place that can make a hell of heaven and a heaven of hell. The ability to reframe the context is, I believe, one of the most powerful sources of inner strength. For example, think about a particularly difficult time in your life. How did you cope? Were you able to step back, think about the wider context, about how it was not all bad? I once met someone who had been diagnosed with arthritis at the age of 34. He said there are three main types and his was the least invasive – so of all the types to get his was the one to go for! He seemed to have a far more positive and constructive outlook than I could imagine.

Similarly, when I hear people moaning about something, I always try to say that it is better than the next category of problem. So if someone has been short changed £1, I say "better than £1.01p." This provokes some interesting reactions but usually it stops the moaning!

When in a stressful situation remind yourself when and where you were happiest. Remember an uplifting song or tune. Remind yourself of close relationships. Try to see the funny side. Concentrate on a much less stressful situation. If someone is interpersonally objectionable, remind yourself of your unique qualities. If you are not certain what they are – what are you doing from tomorrow to ask people to tell you what they are? You may be surprised about just how valued you are. It's the things people don't tell you that you need to know. So ask your trusted advisers and family for their opinions.

Reframe the context

Don't get "locked on transmit" about yourself.
Others are even more interesting

Have you met people who are not listening? Have you ever witnessed a dialogue of the deaf? It seems as though some are so keen for you to know something – they never notice their complete monopolisation of the interaction. They also fail to appreciate they are revealing their own insecurities. There is little perception of their impact on others or that others can see straight through them.

But you don't do that. After all, you have the maturity, and confidence to smile to yourself and consider why people feel so compelled to project themselves in this way – and to the exclusion of input.

I am reminded of a TV advertisement for a car. Four "type A" personality, thrusting young men in suits are in the gym boasting to each other except one, who remains silent but attentive. He gives them a lift in his car. The others realise that it is better than their cars. One of them asked the driver "….and what was it you said you do?" After a pause: "I didn't" came the reply.

The next time you are confronted by someone who is locked on transmit, ask them what sort of feedback they normally ask for regarding their impact on others or in social situations. Be prepared for silence.

By asking others about themselves you can gain invaluable insight into what makes them tick and how you should frame your own interaction with them. By mirroring their choice of words / concepts you will communicate on their wavelength and they will probably find you far more intriguing, influential and compelling.

Don't get "locked on transmit"
about yourself.
Others are even more
interesting

Choose wisely

Take some time to understand the real meaning of "best choice." If you only pursue the cheapest option you need to allow some additional margin for the risk you carry. So that means accommodating a slightly larger budget. And if you can afford to do that, you can afford to pay more in the first place.

I find cultural differences are interesting: I have met quite a few English people who will boast about buying a pen at the cheapest price. That is a good deal, a wise decision. I have also met Germans and Swiss who will say they bought an expensive pen, knowing that their Meisterstück will last a lifetime.

So whatever your choice, make sure it is fit for purpose. However tempting something or even someone may appear – if it is not right – it's not right. We need to be informed. So do we do this from a rational, factual basis? Or, from a more emotional or instinctive basis? How do we weigh the balance of these sometimes conflicting perspectives? Some people have great self-awareness. They know how to listen to rationality and emotion and balance the two. Invariably they will say "My choice is right for me." Or "I know I have made the right decision because of ......" More often than we admit, buying decisions are made for emotional reasons. This applies in personal and professional life. All the data is then used to substantiate the emotional decision that's already made.

By all means be spontaneous in your personal decisions – but know when it is the right time to be so. And keep the balance right. After all, few people would advocate an obviously frivolous choice that was full of risk.

Choose wisely

Live a good honourable life.
Then when you get older, look back and
you will be able to enjoy it a second time

In business I have been involved with corporate ethics policies and codes of conduct. Searching for the simplest way to help employees recognise situations, we said "Think: if you do something will you feel bad? How would you feel if it appeared in the press? Would you have any concern if others were aware of it?" We wanted people to add an ethical dimension to their business decisions.

One can apply these principles to a whole life philosophy. By behaving in an ethical manner you can reflect with ease and some satisfaction knowing that you did the right thing. This concept connects with our earlier discussion on doing the right thing. It provides calm confidence and strength. It enables you to lay decisions to rest without the need to revisit them.

One of the advantages of age it that experience normally brings wisdom. I think people who live an ethical, honourable life become wiser faster and their wisdom develops further. This of course contributes to their sense of purpose, calmness and strength. They find it easier to say "no" calmly and reasonably as well as "yes."

A great example of this was where a senior person was making an unreasonable request of someone. The person on the receiving end simply could not do what was asked – it was impossible for several reasons. So he very calmly replied: "I understand and support what you want. But it cannot be done. While this may create a problem for you; I have no choice." His calm unshakable demeanour clearly indicated that "no" meant "no."

Live a good honourable life.
Then when you get older,
look back and you
will be able to enjoy it
a second time

Money talks; wealth whispers

I think this one came from an advertisement for a Swiss bank. I love its understated message. It uses a pin to burst the balloon of brash conspicuous consumption. So while everyone can see the car you drive and the watch on your wrist, no one can see how much equity you have in your house. Or whether you have a second home or a third one and a yacht moored on its private jetty.

By "under-playing" one's hand, one creates a certain enigma and curiosity. Also, by resisting the temptation to boast, you can smile to yourself as you deploy your resources for the longer term, with more lasting value than transient consumption.

So the next time you experience a brash person who is intent on showing you their latest Rolex, think about how an extra few thousand pounds off the mortgage will pay dividends longer term. There will always be those who say they can easily afford both but my experience of truly wealthy people is that they don't score points. They don't need to.

Understatement can send a far more powerful message. I recall a man enjoying a coffee at the quay-side café in Mahon, wearing very informal casual clothes. He passed the time of day with friends and acquaintances some of whom joked with him regarding his rather faded deck shoes before he crossed the road and walked up onto his £3m Sunseeker yacht. Yet somehow he valued the jokes and friendship more than the boat.

For those with inner strength, wealth is always far more than money. And having money doesn't make you better than the person next to you.

Money talks;
wealth whispers

Money doesn't change people, it reveals them

There is nothing wrong with making and having money. I think most people would agree that unless you work very very hard, you don't get any at all. So a sense of justice comes from fair reward for honest work.

There will always be those whose reward appears excessive – that has always been the case. But as wave upon wave of banking scandals swept the City of London through the summer of 2012, many felt it was out of control. Greed had gained the upper hand. The potential for high reward usually carries with it a moral test: can the person pursue success ethically such that the reward is fairly earned – however huge it may be?

Some people get rich through other means – a few even win the lottery. Perhaps the relegation of previous financial prudence reveals their true personality. In their more carefree world, some people don't mind upsetting others if they can spend their way out of a problem. Some people relive childhood playground behaviour when they get rich – the "look at me" syndrome. The mark of people with real strength and maturity is that wealth brings out the best in them – independence of thought without arrogance. Humility and listening skills should be independent of financial status. TV programmes such as "The secret millionaire" showed how meaning was more important than money.

The rise of compliance and regulation may not have been so necessary if people had had a stronger moral compass. Had that been the case, maybe personal ethics and conduct would have been valued and policed by organisations and colleagues.

Money doesn't change people,
it reveals them

Swimming with Piranha makes you hungry

Human nature is tribal and affilliative. People want to belong. By all means associate with whoever you like and feel part of the team. It is great to belong. But don't belong just for the sake of it. Be aware of who you associate with and why.

People with inner strength have a certain independence as well as choosing to belong to various groups of friends. They recognise that if they swim with certain types: "piranhas" it is inevitable that they will adopt some of their habits and tendencies. If everyone has to have that expensive style, then to belong – you need it too. So note your choices: are you doing things because you want to do them or because everyone else is doing them?

Consider the cost of living if everyone in a group has to have numerous expensive badges of office: the expensive car, watch, accessories, suits, holidays and so on. Everything in moderation! So just be aware that by associating with obsessives, you run the risk of going with them and becoming a hungry Piranha yourself. Some never have enough of what they don't really need. Let it be your choice not someone else's. That way you stay in control and your strength is enhanced.

It can take courage to go against the flow and it may even be ill-advised in certain circumstances. But a full awareness of what is going on helps people to make fully informed decisions. That way they avoid becoming fashion victims whose mindless feeding frenzies eventually culminate in the question "what was that all about?"

Swimming with Piranha
makes you hungry

Spanish proverb says it is the best table cloth that gets the stain, but it will have lived, been enjoyed

Have you noticed some people buy precious things only to have them for "best use" only? Consequently they hardly ever get used and eventually they go out of fashion or become obsolete in other ways.

This cultural gem is all about using prized possessions and enjoying them to the full. The proof of something being used to the full is that it "gets the stain." In other words it is the frequency of use and the level of enjoyment that brings the risk of the stain! Compare this to the story of the beetroot earlier.

The other piece of advice contained in this quotation is about being OK with the stain. It is about accepting that the perfect tablecloth – or any other object cannot stay in pristine condition forever. If it did – you could not have enjoyed it. Being at ease with this is a tall order for some people. Having a sense of perspective includes the ability to accept that things wear out and get stained through use. Enjoyment is all about use, so there is a trade-off.

Maybe part of inner strength is about defining the true meaning of value. Does the tablecloth have intrinsic value or does its value reside in its ability to bring people together and have a good time through good meals, good conversation and fun? .....Food for thought.

A family friend once said "Rather than us coming to your place and bringing our children (who might trash your house), why don't you come over to ours – it's been trashed already!"

Spanish proverb says
it is the best table cloth
that gets the stain,
but it will have lived,
been enjoyed

Get a good fruit bowl and fill it well; that will improve your diet more than most

In our fast-paced, fast-forward world, the rise of convenience foods marches on, year by year. I have noticed the supermarkets steadily substituting good quality basic products with "value-added" processed products allegedly to save time. So instead of selling a lettuce, they offer a gas-filled, pre-washed, pre-selected selection of cut lettuce pieces. Unfortunately as soon as the inert gas is out of the bag, the contents go brown in 12 hours!

Perhaps one of the few exceptions is fresh fruit. Apart from the obvious health benefits of eating more fruit, having a well-stocked bowl acts as a focal point. See how at work or at home a good fruit bowl can become a social thing – bringing people together.

By eating less junk food and more fruit, one's health, weight, skin and physique will improve over a period of time. Improved health contributes to a more cheerful optimistic disposition. And that of course builds confidence and strength. You may think this now sounds far-fetched. Perhaps it is. But try it anyway!

A former colleague used to use fruit as a pattern interrupt to break the log-jam in meetings. During tough negotiations he would bring out a tangerine and peel it slowly. He would offer pieces to people before calling an adjournment to wash his hands. Sometimes people would follow into the washroom. Surprisingly, this simple change of pace and the injection of a pause into the meeting frequently worked wonders. The change of setting enabled a new conversation.

Get a good fruit bowl
and fill it well;
that will improve your diet
more than most.

Desire for status reflects lack of self esteem; pursue only material wealth and you will never be satisfied

If you are still reading, my guess is that you will have been expecting a quotation like this one. I think one of the defining characteristics of strong people is that they know who they are, they are comfortable with who they are and they don't need to say "look at me, look at me." Their self esteem is high and this brings confidence.

The problem with pursuing only material wealth is that the sky really is the limit. Hence the quotation earlier: "know when to stop" and the discussion on the law of diminishing returns. The most telling point about diminishing returns in the context of pursuing materialism is that the effort required to get up to the next level becomes more and more. The danger is that it becomes all-consuming to the exclusion of everything else. People who follow that path stand out as rather unfortunate people who have "lost the plot." Their quest for status actually has the opposite effect. My observation is that respect comes from sincerity, integrity, making and keeping promises and delivery. And that is about saying what you mean, meaning what you say and delivering promises in this uncertain post-Lehman world.

What is status anyway? Could it be that the greatest status of all comes from high self-esteem? If so — it is more an internal state of mind than a physical embodiment. Who has the higher status: someone who is Loathed, "Loaded" or Loved?

Desire for status reflects
lack of self esteem;
pursue only material wealth
and you will never be satisfied

When you lose, make sure you don't lose the lesson

It is inevitable that we all have setbacks. An earlier quotation is helpful in terms of "get over it." The value of losing – something, an argument, someone - is what it teaches us. If we do not learn the lesson and remember it, the opportunity is completely wasted.

Instead of getting angry or emotionally hijacked by the bad experience – try to collect as much learning as possible, given the circumstances. Always try and make sure you don't lose the lesson. That way, you stand the strongest chance of never repeating the same mistake or loss.

Some might call this learning from experience. Others might say a fool deserves to make the same mistake twice. It is surprising however that even rational, intelligent people get derailed by their emotions and fail to learn the full lesson when they have setbacks.

The lesson is not just the immediate impact of the loss. It includes all the peripheral and related impacts. The medium and long term impact, the impact on other opportunities and other people, the opportunity cost and so on. In the current austerity, euro crisis et al, the application of learning is all the more important – you cannot borrow your way out of a problem any more.

The very activity of ensuring one learns the lesson has a great strengthening quality about it. It normally stops people moaning or moving towards paralysis and it stiffens their resolve. Those who are determined to learn the lesson are usually calmer people with more confidence who strangely don't have to learn many lessons very often. The more they learn, the greater their inner strength.

When you lose, make sure you don't lose the lesson

Big hat, no cattle

I hope this American quotation needs no explanation. Perhaps instead we should explore what causes people to behave in a way that provokes this observation. It may be their ego, wishing to project a bigger image, their insecurity or just a misunderstanding. Or it could be simple old fashioned ambition grown to exaggeration. Whatever the reason, normally the person with the metaphorical big hat doesn't realise that others know the truth – there are no cattle. The result is a rapid erosion of credibility until the hat is consigned to the waste bin.

Some people like to play power games on the assumption that all power is taken not given. While this may be true, it does require verification. I have seen people meet their career trap door by acting ultra vires – without authority. It therefore remains important to obtain and retain executive sponsorship and "air cover." These days, governance has never been more important. Those who display exemplary ethics, compliance and stakeholder management are at last getting noticed. That's how it should have been all along.

In social situations there will always be people trying to impress. In particular they may boast about things that cannot be verified. I like to watch their eyes as they search for a response to my questions which show some understanding of the subject but give no clue regarding belief or my own situation. People who look away while answering usually have some difficulty with what they are saying. Also, people who tell you things you really don't need to know may have interesting motives – as discussed before. Learning to recognise these signals helps one maintain a healthy independence of view. Remember: cow in field may not be all it seems.

Big hat,
no cattle

Action conquers fear

It is well accepted that fear and anxiety can cause procrastination, indecision and paralysis. I believe there are times when taking action – even if it turns out to be wrong, helps to overcome fear. At least taking action enables people to assess what they are doing, take stock and then corrective action.

I once had "the pleasure" of an army assault course – against the clock. The final challenge was a 3 or 4 metre wooden plank suspended by four chains, one per corner. Beneath was a 2 metre deep vat of green slime. Those who hesitated were tipped into the slime because putting their weight slowly onto the plank caused the opposite end to tip up. However, running onto it meant that as the far end rose up, one's next stride came down to meet it. It was like running along a children's see-saw. The far end dipped into the slime as one's final stride stepped onto solid ground. Thankfully I did not need to be hosed down that day. The challenge was counter-intuitive and rewarded those who grasped the nettle.

Think also about how you feel before diving into a cold swimming pool. The determination to swim straight away at a brisk pace is the best way to reduce the trepidation and reluctance to dive. The worst thing to do is dive in then freeze and complain. If nothing else, swim to the side and get out as soon as possible. I hope you will appreciate both the practical and metaphorical advice here. It was gained from speaking to and observing people who have overcome fear. Or who at the very least can "feel the fear and do it anyway" to quote the title of a book.

Action conquers fear

If you treat people like enemies, you'll get a war

Caution is one thing but innate and unnecessary suspicion are quite another. Being generous in one's interactions is a confidence boosting benefit. I have watched people who smile at others on first meeting having a demonstrably better interaction. They are more appealing, more interesting. Conversely, those who look cold and uninviting are less welcoming and people are not attracted to them.

Suspicion and feelings that the other person is out to trick someone can lead to a downward spiral in a relationship. This can become a self-fulfilling prophesy and before long people are treating each other like enemies. They look for problems and evidence to fit their preconceived ideas. Slowly but surely you get a war. Those with inner strength have the confidence to give others the benefit of the doubt. They make up their own minds.

Think back to your school days. Did you ever witness people falling out for no real reason? Were small differences ever exaggerated to an unreasonable extent? Just as this can lead to playground fights, in later life people can harbour grudges that take years or even decades to heal. Taking an opportunity to check why someone has a particular view, can help maintain a healthy relationship. This helps you manage multiple stakeholders – which is particularly helpful at work.

We have already discussed the notion of not letting a little dispute damage a great friendship. This can apply equally to a current friendship or one that has yet to develop.

If you treat people like enemies,
you'll get a war

We don't stop playing games because we get older; we get old because we stop playing games

Busy people must make time for fun. Life is so full of serious matters that it is easy to forget the light-hearted side. As with so many things it is important to retain a sense of balance. Seeing the funny side of things, being able to step back and laugh and retaining one's sense of humour are ever more important in a pressurised life. Similarly, having fun can be a wise investment and escape.

And it goes further. By keeping in touch with youth culture and popular recreation, one benefits from a wider set of perspectives. This can be instructive and add to one's contextual understanding. I suspect you have met people who appeared old and "timed-out" at 55 and others who had the attitude and vigour of a 25 year old at the same age. One of the brightest, most incisive people I met was actually over the age of 90.

Some of the strongest people I have observed, have been those who despite the passing years, have gone to great efforts to keep up to date, stay in touch, have a wide network of young and old and retain a keen sense of adventure - even a little childish mischief. Laughter improves health and strengthens work and social networks. It makes difficult situations easier.

Of course my reference to "playing games" is the innocent sort – not political manipulation, not being devious or of low integrity.

We don't stop playing games
because we get older;
we get old because
we stop playing games

If you have to fight, first make sure you will win

All too often I think people get hijacked emotionally and feel they must fight something or even someone "as a matter of principle." Unfortunately, their inability to step back and assess the situation in the cold light of day means they make ill-advised decisions. When faced with the choice of settling or losing, most people would opt to settle. However people get dug-in and can find it harder and harder to climb out of the hole they are digging.

People I have observed with remarkable composure, typically have had rapier–like focus. They are experienced in weighing up situations. They know which battles to fight and which to walk away from. They move on emotionally. They never have any second thoughts or "what if?" lingering doubts about those they walk away from. Instead, they devote all their attention to how they can win those battles they choose to fight. These are few and far between. Through planning, preparation and resource allocation they then ensure they have as many allies as possible. Then and only when they are confident of winning, do they enter the fray. With calm resolve, they sweep all before them and I have to say, it looks effortless.

There is a lesson here. It speaks of wide angle vision, forward planning, stakeholder management, reputation management, the presentation of self, leadership, emotional control and personal resolve. It also acts as a warning not to fight unless you are really sure you can win. No one likes defeat and no one likes to be regarded as defeated. Learning these lessons builds a reputation for inner strength.

If you have to fight,
first make sure you will win

There are those who listen
and those who wait to speak

This quotation has a similarity to the earlier one regarding some people being "locked on transmit." It is however subtly different because those who only wait to speak have a tendency not to listen. For example where there is a pause in the conversation, they launch into their monologue which increasingly bears little resemblance to the previous flow or theme of conversation. This is a fruitful source or theme for comedy writers. There are two problems: first while there might appear to be a dialogue, there isn't. There are two parallel monologues: a dialogue of the deaf. Unlike the person who is locked on transmit, this person fills gaps in the interchange with their own blocks of speaking. Secondly, the problem with not listening is that the semblance of communication breaks down and the person on the receiving end is more aggrieved than in a situation of "transmit only."

This quotation is trying to divide humanity into those people who really pay attention to the people they are with, versus those who are only interested in their own agenda – getting their point across whether the recipient likes it or not, whether they are paying attention or not.

Most people with inner strength pause before making their point. They are clear and succinct. They listen and their conversation develops, benefiting from the interchange. As you might expect, they are influential and they will pursue an argument to persuade people. But they check to see the extent of their persuasive progress.

They know that a bore can be a fool and a bore who does not listen is even more foolish.

There are those who listen
and those who wait to speak

Appreciate what you have while you have it

Too many see faults when they have things or relationships and remember only good things when they are gone. Many assume their income stream, such as salary, bonus, benefits let alone health, will be with them forever. Many also assume annual increases with everyone getting richer and richer. In some cultures, "bonus" isn't bonus at all – it is salary in drag. There, the entitlement mentality of an inflationary increase was never in doubt. This is however much less evident today.

In relationships, familiarity breeds contempt and where people fail to invest in the quality of a relationship, they sometimes are surprised when the other party simply walks away. This could be a supplier/customer relationship; a friendship or a family or marital relationship.

The ability to step back and appreciate things and relationships "in the round" is a rare skill. The ability to put aside the negatives – recognising that nothing is perfect, is very rare. Appreciating qualities, despite the disadvantages enables people to concentrate on what is important and to show their appreciation of those qualities. That actually strengthens the relationship and diminishes the very issues that detract from it.

There is strength to be gained from appreciating what one has and valuing it against the context of not having any of it. The more one appreciates "things" the more one understands their transient nature. Relationships can endure much longer and have a high intangible value. Should we value time from the perspective of an expensive watch or the time people are prepared to devote to us?

Appreciate what you have
while you have it

Many people see what you appear to be; few experience what you really are

They say life is a stage and one is seen by many people every day. Many see what you appear to be and they form their own conclusions from countless signals – whether verbal or non-verbal. However very few people directly experience your decisions and actions. Many of us have met people who have a reputation that is different from the reality.

My observation of those with inner strength is that they have a certain irreverence or disdain for image management. They are never so insecure as to worry much about what others think about them. Yet their very state of independence creates an image itself. They acquire a reputation for unflappable confidence and calmness in stressful situations. Their personal values create a reputation for consistency and integrity. By having a recognisable personal brand, their reputation enhances the real-life experience.

Having a reputation that assists, clearly has great value. So it should be guarded and kept intact. Reputation goes much much further than one's direct contact with others. It features in many subtle ways in the widest network of conversations.

Having a good reputation is obviously helpful but it can be lost very quickly: "you are only as good as your last mistake" as some would say. Those who can step back and look at themselves appreciate the value of their reputation and what it may require to rebuild it.

Many people see
what you appear to be;
few experience
what you really are

When the curtain comes down
it's time to get off the stage

In the great succession of projects that constitute a lifetime, most have a defined start, middle and end. Why is it then that so many people cannot see the end or have either a blind spot or go into denial? If something is dead: an object, a relationship, a role, a person – it's helpful to understand when this really is the end. No one should keep going back to see whether it is coming back to life or continue with the deceased as if nothing has changed. If it has gone, it's gone – so walk away.

Of course, it takes both humility and strength to do this. But people gain credit for doing so. By recognising situations for what they really are, we can move on and live a different life – hopefully enriched by what was, but never held back by what might have been.

There's nothing worse than someone in denial about their fall from prominence. The acting analogy is particularly instructive. No one would dream of carrying on acting when the stage curtain has come down. Recognising that "this dog has had its day" can be motivating for people to find their next project or challenge. The challenge comes hardest to those who define themselves by what they do rather than who they are.

The real skill of course is to plan ahead, to have contingencies and to recognise the signs that the curtain might come down. I was once told "the effective MBA always knows where their next job is coming from – they are always on the lookout." Recognising situations for what they could develop into gives great strength because one can stay in control. That way, you happen to the world rather than the world happening to you.

When the curtain comes down
it's time to get off the stage

Life is a series of projects

That is to say it is not a continuum, not a straight line and not predictable. Once people accept this and start to get comfortable with it, a whole wave of strength flows towards them. Life is also a series of mandates. One is given a mandate to do something, to have something, to develop something. Or to have a role to play, be it in the family, among friends or at work. And just as families evolve and friends come and go, so jobs can come and go.

At work, the only way to take control of one's own career is to understand that work is a series of projects and mandates. My observation of those most comfortable with this are people who say "while I am here I want interesting work, I will develop my own marketable skills, I'll stay up to date and one day I will leave." They also add: "I may leave because you tell me to or because I decide to but either way I will be ready any time."

Outside work, a project approach can be helpful as a means of ensuring that tasks get done, longer projects progress and also to recognise that nothing endures forever. This in turn helps people to appreciate what they have while they have it. For example recognising that we are all mortal helps people to get the most out of family relationships while they can. Conversely those who cannot come to terms with the death of a parent, have frequently lived their own lives in denial of the inevitable and have made no emotional preparation.

My observation of people who choose what to do and then get things done is that their output orientation creates strength in themselves and those around them.

Life is a series of projects

Concentrate on the essential few things that must be achieved

It is easy to get overwhelmed by the sheer volume of day to day tasks. Recognising that work will always expand to fill the time available, it follows that there will always be more to do and therefore insufficient time to do it. I am not only referring to one's occupation. This could be house work, DIY or gardening, home administration, managing one's family or holiday planning. It is therefore absolutely essential that one has the courage and strength to say "no" as well as "yes." One of the strongest people I met once said that stress is caused by people themselves because they cannot say "no" – to colleagues, the boss, their friends or themselves! Instead of reprioritising and helping others to realise that one of the current tasks now has to stop in order to address the new one, they take on more and then fail to deliver.

The act of prioritising and re-prioritising builds clarity and strength and de-stresses one's life. So by concentrating on the essential few things that must be done, there is better focus, there are fewer distractions and the results are delivered more easily. This is contingent on one having the courage to let go and decline to do the non essential things. And – to recognise that changing priorities may well mean that what was once essential no longer is. Know the difference between what's urgent and what's important.

It is better to have a reputation for delivery of the essential few than for erratic delivery of the many. The more things one politely declines to do, the easier it gets and the easier it becomes to concentrate on the essential few.

Concentrate on
the essential few things
that must be achieved

Context is everything, learn how to see it

Whenever I have been perplexed at someone's behaviour, through an unexpected reaction, I have always returned to this advice. It came from a former boss of mine. When faced with a highly charged emotional manager, I had been briefed that she had a personal crisis outside work that explained the apparent irrationality.

Similarly, people's prejudices, culture, education, financial situation and health all have a bearing on their behaviour. By understanding the viewpoint of others, one can understand more of why they have the view they have. This helps people get to a better interaction, a better outcome. Try to see the rational, irrational, emotional, political then the pragmatic point of view.

So if you see someone about to wrestle a stranger to the ground, is it an unprovoked attack or are they pulling them out of the trajectory of a piece of falling masonry above? While this is an unlikely example, there are many others which provoke a re-assessment. The way different cultures address ethical dilemmas can be instructive.

Imagine you are driving a car but you have a crash that is your fault. Your passenger's testimony can exonerate you – would they testify to defend you: if they were a stranger, a friend, a member of your family, your spouse?

At the pub, imagine you feel it is clearly the other person's turn to buy the drinks. They avoid this. How would your opinion of them change if you knew: they were deeply in debt; they were very well off but absent minded; they thought the drinks far too expensive, or they had bought two rounds just before you arrived?

Context is everything, learn how to see it

A Roman emperor said
People don't change, only the date

A former colleague once said to me "the higher they get, the shorter the trousers." This took some explanation but he meant the more senior an executive gets, the more she or he behaves like they did in the primary school playground. When I came across the emperor's quotation, I was struck by the similarity. I was also struck by the wisdom reaching back 2000 years.

Perhaps there is a certain naivety that expects older people or more experienced and educated people to behave with ever greater rationality. However, they too have emotions. Where they display particularly driven or obsessive characteristics, they may actually display ever - more irrational behaviour. Once one understands this counter-intuitive tendency, one is prepared for the unexpected or at least for the unusual!

My observation of people with inner strength is that they accept and recognise that others may behave with low integrity or may manipulate people and situations for their own gain. After all, cow in field may not be all it seems. However it is the ability to recognise situations that prepares and equips us for a more influential interaction and a better outcome. Forewarned is forearmed.

So instead of being disappointed at the re-appearance of playground tactics, we should learn to recognise them throughout life. They will be there long after we are gone. History can teach us some valuable lessons.

A Roman emperor said
People don't change,
only the date

The best things in life aren't things

In our fast forward world, the emphasis on material possessions and wealth seems to grow each year. Every so often, someone says "stop" and goes against the flow. In 2005, a comic rant against consumerism hit the pre-Christmas best seller list. The book was called "Is it me or is everything shit?" Many people thought it was a silly season joke. However it remained on the best seller list for months.

The problem with "things" is that familiarity brings contempt and comparison brings envy. Eventually things fade, become obsolete or can be taken away from you. You may have heard or even experienced the story of the man who was delighted with his new car until he discovered that his neighbour just got a better one.

As a child, I asked my parents why they were spending so much money sending their two sons to a private school. There was never any free/easy money about at home. "Make do and mend" was alive in our house. The answer was "because of all the things we could give you, education is the one thing that cannot easily be taken away from you." This was profound and of course reflected their context of having lived through and indeed served in the second world war. I didn't realise it at the time but post-war austerity was the context.

If the best things aren't things, what are they? Probably a lot of things we take for granted, until that is - we no longer have them. Personal freedom, privacy, friendship, security, love, support, our personal support network, a sense of belonging, health, vitality, confidence, cheerful optimism, happiness, mastery, autonomy, purpose and dare I say it: inner strength.

The best things in life
aren't things

Once a year,
go somewhere you have never been before

Pattern interrupts are always a good wake-up call. They cause us to stop, take stock and think about why we are doing something. It is very easy to get into a weekly, monthly or annual routine and then wonder where the years went. If we accept that travel broadens the mind, then this quotation is encouraging us to broaden by creating new experiences. Naturally, bringing back the learning is an important facet of any new experience.

There is enough value in this quotation to apply it to many physical places such as holidays and travel. However I think it can apply much more widely. This is because it is advocating stretching the envelope of experience. Pushing new boundaries could also be about personal endurance, resilience, standing up for what you believe in, trying harder to see someone else's point of view. The point is about broadening experience and learning from it. This adds to personal wisdom and strength. When you go to a different place, go somewhere new in your mind too.

Sometimes people need to push themselves to break routine, to force something new to happen. In a busy life it is easy to adopt a routine in which one does not expect disruption or change.

Expectation is an interesting angle on this. Sometimes the most surprising things can come from where one least expects them. Having an open mind brings further value. I remember nonchalantly accepting an invitation to a student afternoon tea party in a friend's study. Little did I know that my future wife would also walk into that room.

Once a year,
go somewhere you have
never been before

Indian proverb says the first day a guest, the second day a guest, the third day a calamity

Have you ever had this experience? You invite some friends or family members over for a long week end and polite conversation lasts about 24 hours. Then the interactions change such that by the third day the inhibitions are lost and arguments can start!

So having guests requires renewal and a focus or purpose. This in turn puts considerable pressure on the host. The quotation at least alerts the host to the magnitude of the task. And if after consideration, one decides the task is too great – then maybe now is not the best time to invite people for several days. The pre-emptive solution is to shorten their visit or change the dates.

People with inner strength appear to me to have the foresight to predict what could go wrong with guest relationships. They appear to pre-empt awkward situations before they appear. In the event of things deteriorating, they handle them with great interpersonal skill. This is thanks to their emotional intelligence and ability to step back and see a variety of perspectives.

Perhaps another aspect of this wisdom from India, is the notion of each day the visitors being a "guest." Perhaps if they were playing a different role such as helper, or equal partner or reciprocal contributor – the calamity would be averted. The notion of "guest" implies that the host is acting as hotelier and servant. This is a recipe for "get it yourself" after the tenth request for something from the fridge! Being a guest is not a passive role; it requires a contribution in kind. So calmly agree some ground rules.

Indian proverb says
the first day a guest,
the second day a guest,
the third day a calamity

What are dreams for if not to come true?

With all the rationality in this collection of quotations, you might regard this one as a breath of fresh air and emotion. Yet I see no contradiction: I have seen great strength in people who focus on their goal, whether it is a simple task or a lifetime ambition. As we have discussed before, there will be adversity for sure. This is simply a test of one's resolve. The dream may prove difficult, illusive or even impossible. However for those with the strength to go on, their dreams persist to be achieved. Then prioritisation becomes the governing factor. The empty person is someone who has a dream but is not prepared to do anything about it and yet won't drop the idea or change it.

I have met some very determined people. Some so overtly "in your face" that they were obnoxious in the extreme. Others were clearly obsessed and were prepared to sweep everything in their path to get what they wanted. But those I admire the most take a balanced view, balance the risks and step by step effectively progress to completion. What is so amusing is the shock on the faces of others who could not see the result coming. They think it is by magic (or cheating).

Whether you favour the tortoise or the hare, there is more than one way to run a race. I have seen people motivated and sustained by their dream, especially where they involved others and made private and public commitments to their personal network. Everyone knew what was going to be achieved eventually; no one wanted failure so they helped and supported the person on their route to ever-more-certain achievement.

What are dreams for
if not to come true?

Take regular exercise and do everything possible to get the right amount of sleep

Have you ever wondered how some people appear to have stamina, endurance and can cope with significant pressure? A common denominator appears to be their approach to physical health. They know their limits and insist on a balance in their physical life. They know long term sleep deprivation is very damaging. They also take exercise in an appropriate way. I am not a fan of the endorphin-junkie approach which starts every day with 2 hours in the gym. That seems to be bordering on obsession − unless you are training for a marathon. I have been told that in normal life, walking or some other form of light heart strain every day is a very good way of keeping the balance. It also causes you to spend time away from everything else. Try the stairs instead of the lift. While no one can lead a business from behind a desk, try not to fly long haul every week.

Someone who overcame stress at work was told to go for a 30 minute walk, outside, every lunch time. He was under strict instruction to end any meeting to keep to this regime. He would calmly apologise for leaving a meeting on account of another engagement and would walk out to meet the daily requirement. The interesting by-product was that by saying "no" to meetings with no clear end and by leaving to take a walk, it became easier to assert what he felt was right. The world of work reduced to a more manageable part of his healthier life.

Meanwhile the obsessives, the machos and the fearful carried on and their lives outside work fell into disrepair, their health suffered, and when they reached their materialist peak, many realised no one was with them or behind them.

Take regular exercise
and do everything possible
to get the right amount
of sleep

Learn to say "no" with calm confidence as well as "yes"

We know it can be difficult giving a message the recipient does not want to hear. But do we stop to think how much worse the message is when people feel badly let down? I firmly believe that saying "yes" and then returning to try and explain that it is really a "no" is far more difficult.

Your daughter is stranded at a bus stop; there is no bus. She calls asking to be picked up. You say yes and then don't show up. What sort of a message does that send? If however you need to educate her on self-sufficiency and remind her of the timetable, pointing out that the next bus will be along in 30 minutes and it would take you 20 to get to her – she can wait for an extra 10.

If your boss asks you to do something but you already feel at maximum stretch, instead of saying "yes" do you say "my capacity is full, so in accepting this, which of the previous tasks do you want me to stop working on?" For some reason many people have difficulty with this. Yet it is an essential step to building inner strength. Interestingly, the more this reply is spoken, the easier it gets. The more the boss is encouraged to think about workload prioritisation, the more valuable the employee becomes. It's all about focus.

I have also found people "shopping around" for the answer they want. They will ask the same question in different ways as a means of trying to get what they want. I once heard someone reply: "You have asked a perfectly reasonable question and I hope you have found I gave a perfectly reasoned answer. Now then, what part of "no" don't you understand?" Firmness was required.

Learn to say "no"
with calm confidence
as well as "yes"

Recognise that almost all worries are about things that don't happen

Human nature is to fear not so much the worst but actually worse than the worst. Many people never prepare for the worst and hope for the best. They actively assume worse than the worst and fail to prepare for anything because they are so debilitated by the tricks of their mind. But in reality, nothing is as bad (or actually as good) as it seems at the time.

Because our minds can play tricks on us, we assume that the worst possible outcome is going to happen. But in reality this very seldom occurs. Anxiety is internal, it is abstract and it often tries to deny the objective facts. When summoned to the headmaster's study did you anticipate: an enquiry, a congratulation, a flogging or an expulsion? Or did you simply not know? – in which case speculation is no more than that: speculation. My brother once heard the following announcement from an airline pilot: "If any passenger understands the complexities of computers, would they please make themselves known to a member of the cabin crew." As fellow passengers went white with fear, my brother was escorted to the cockpit to find a bored captain wanting advice on which PC to buy his son. (Note this was pre 9-11, when access to airliner cockpits was quite common.)

Even when confronted by very serious and major personal disasters, the most important determinant of outcomes is one's attitude and approach to what happened. When Christopher Reeve (the actor who played Superman) had his spinal injury, he and his wife spent the rest of his life campaigning for the disabled. Most would agree that his legacy is greater for this work than for his film career.

Recognise that almost all
worries are about
things that don't happen

Everything in moderation, especially the moderation

Naturally there are limits to rationality and there are times when spontaneity and fun simply have to predominate. One cannot be cool and calculating all the time. So as with so many things, a sense of balance is essential for happiness and a well balanced life. And maybe additional strength comes from having the confidence to be utterly spontaneous against a background of knowing what one's limits are.

For example if you manage your financial affairs well, buying something on a whim may have great sentimental value, especially when you know you can afford it. Even wasting money at a casino may be a good decision once in a while simply for the fun of it – but against a background of knowing what is sensible.

In other words, don't stifle creativity, spontaneity and fun by being too sensible too often. After all it's the things we don't do that we regret. The guiding principle of this quotation is to know the context in which you are operating. What might appear utterly extravagant could be perfectly rational in a different context.

You see someone sipping a drink on the stern of a sparkling new motoryacht. Have they won the lottery rollover? Are they billionaires? Have they chartered it for a week and blown their life savings? Or have they chartered it for a week with 6 other friends – having saved up for it for 10 years? Only you can decide the appropriateness of your decisions but personal resilience and strength enables you to explore the wild side – in moderation of course.

Everything in moderation, especially the moderation

There is more to life than increasing its speed

While there are some advantages of packing as much as possible into your schedule, there is a growing body of opinion saying "Stop the world, I want to get off." In France there is the campaign for slow food as an antidote to the 15 minute fast food break. Following the 2005 survey that claimed UK couples spent 17 minutes per day in meaningful conversation, a 2006 survey alleged working parents spent a daily average of just 19 minutes with their young children. By 2012, excessive use of Twitter and Facebook were treatable addictions.

Spinning faster and faster reduces opportunities for enjoying the simple pleasures of life especially those that have no cost. The addictive spiral is therefore a vortex of: work harder, do more, spend more, have more, work more, earn more. A CEO I once knew said that for every promotion he had, his hourly rate had gone down. Another problem with the "more more faster faster" approach is its inherent superficiality. Can people really appreciate something that is experienced in a fleeting moment? Or are they fashion victims who waste their resources? Those with the courage and strength to follow a different route make time for the simpler things as a means of keeping a balance. They argue that going faster misses what life is all about.

Conversation, relationships and investing in one's network need time which is a rare commodity today. Having the strength to decide what your life is about rather than get caught up in a mouse wheel is one of your big decisions. A diamond studded mouse wheel is still a mouse wheel.

There is more to life than
increasing its speed

The world as we see it is only the world as we see it. Others may see it very differently

Perhaps it is human nature that we see, think and speak of things in terms of our own frame of reference. We tend not to articulate alternative perspectives. So parochialism prevails. An earlier quotation spoke of "Fog in channel, continent cut off." It is interesting that on the day I am writing this page, there are two demonstrations taking place in the UK. One is against scientific testing using animals. The other is for the complete opposite.

At a concert last week, I found the sound pressure levels too high and yet it was not loud enough for the young man next to me. Whereas the English regard their home as their castle – with absolute privacy within, many Europeans have a name plate next to their door bell. In the UK we tend to recoil from regulation, especially in our homes and gardens but in other countries people welcome restrictions on domestic noise and interference. Whereas any English suburban garden in summer will have weekend lawn mower noise and the smell of barbeques, in Germany both are frowned upon and are verboten on a Sunday. Chewing gum is a national obligation in the USA but it is illegal in Singapore. In Europe we love beef. In India cows are sacred. In China, certain anatomical parts are a culinary delicacy and yet we wince at the thought. In South America Gerbils are also a delicacy – just don't tell your 10 year old daughter.

Understanding alternative perspectives informs our decisions and judgements. This frequently improves interpersonal skill which in turn increases confidence and the strength to take discussions well beyond the superficial.

The world as we see it
is only the world as we see it.
Others may see it
very differently.

Perfection is achieved not when there is nothing more to add but when there is nothing further to take away

Whether it is in conversation, making something, writing or other areas of creativity – many of us have a tendency to think excellence means total coverage. The more the merrier. I remember a geography teacher's comment on my essay that said half way through "Your answer could have begun here for the same mark." Making a clear design statement usually means simplicity of form. "Less is more" is now a well known phrase.

My observation of great communicators is that they speak clearly, simply and actually quite slowly. They understand that people can only really hold up to three ideas at once. They recognise that audiences will probably remember only what they thought about while the speaker was speaking to them. It is the internal conversation with themselves that invokes the real communication.

Strength of conviction is conveyed by using clear simple language. Remember the pause: no one falls asleep in silence. I have witnessed the use of pauses having a far more profound impact than simply adding more and more words.

The next time you are faced by someone who bombards you with verbiage, ask yourself why are they doing this? Perhaps they lack confidence to express themselves simply and succinctly. Maybe they aren't totally in command of their brief and feel they have to resort to bombardment to stifle questions or prove a point. Ask yourself "can I get my point across in 30 seconds or less?" If you can, I am confident you will have people asking for more and you'll draw them in.

Perfection is achieved not
when there is nothing more
to add but when there is
nothing further to take away

If someone tells you something they really don't need
to tell you, ask yourself "Why?"
– the opposite may be true

This quotation builds upon the one about people being
locked on transmit. In social situations there is the inevitable
sizing people up, putting them into pigeon holes and
generally labelling them. People want to know whether the
new acquaintance is "one of us." This sniffing around usually
comprises the exchange of various questions regarding work,
family, where people live, what they drive and where they
spend their holidays. People who have a certain lack of self
esteem or other insecurity sometimes start to exaggerate.
They think that a few white lies don't do any harm. However
they reveal their insecurities by these exaggerations. Those
with inner strength firstly don't need to exaggerate: they
are more comfortable with themselves and life in general.
They don't need to score points. They also know the value
of under-playing their hand. This maintains a certain interest
and desire from others to find out more about such an
interesting person. By asking questions of others, one learns
far more than simply monopolising the conversation oneself.

When people tell you something that is not relevant to the
flow of conversation and strikes you as rather odd – ask
yourself why is this person telling me this ? Is it to impress,
to assert, to show off or is there some other reason? I was
once told such things are more likely to be untrue than true.

If someone tells you something
they really don't need to tell you,
ask yourself "Why?"
— the opposite may be true

It's the things we don't do that we regret

How many times have you heard people say "if only" and then give a range of excuses for inaction. Some will be plausible, some perfectly rational but some will remain excuses. Recognising that life is no rehearsal, the passage of time is a great mechanism to help us make choices – provided we recognise that time is passing in the first place.

This quotation is about reflection on things we don't do. Even when things go wrong, we tend not to regret them. And so we shouldn't, because the learning can ultimately be more valuable. After all, when you lose, you make sure you don't lose the lesson. Was it Shakespeare who said it is better to have loved and lost than not to have loved at all? There is learning in almost all experience. A very entrepreneurial manager once said to me "Much of life is about turning up" – ie being there. Life can be quite serendipitous. Many times I have bumped into people at business and social events who have put me in touch with others. The ability to leverage other peoples' networks can be a real asset.

People tend to regret what might have happened or what might have been. The antidote? – perhaps it is about planning and setting goals regarding what one wants to achieve. So if you want to skipper that 70 foot yacht on the open sea, out of sight of land, break the task down into manageable chunks then set realistic timescales to prepare, train, get experience, get qualified and save up.

It is rarely too late to accomplish something when the motivation is really there. Rather than give up and say "it is too late now..." Strong resilient people challenge themselves by asking "why not?"

It's the things we don't do
that we regret

Nothing is ever as bad or as good as it seems

Earlier in our discussion, I wrote of human nature inventing worries or anxieties about things that rarely happen. Our sense of exaggerated perception plays tricks on us. When in a "bad situation" it may help to assess the reality in a more detached way. Almost always, things are not as bad as they appear. Even from tragedy, good things can come. In professional life I have come across may people who thought their world would end when they faced sudden, unexpected career transition. Almost all of them later got back in touch to say it was a good thing; they are now in more meaningful jobs and are happier and stronger having had the experience. Even those who have not matched their previous earnings have said they are happier. Others not only matched their previous earnings but went well beyond.

Similarly, nothing is as good as it seems. Even the world's most luxurious holiday is a memory and a set of impressive photographs a year or two later. Think about context, why something is "good" in the first place. Will it be eclipsed by something else? Or will it become less relevant with the passage of time? For example, was that ecstatic moment at your first live pop concert something that endured into adulthood? I doubt it.

Time is a great healer when it comes to the perception of difficult or tragic situations. It is also a diluter of the perception of good and great situations. It also serves as a reminder about the law of diminishing returns. Frequently excitement diminishes with familiarity and so people seek bigger thrills to compensate. As with so many areas in life, the real skill is knowing where and when to stop.

Nothing is ever as bad
or as good as it seems

Plan what you can afford before
deciding what you want

In today's fast-forward cultures, "I want it now" and aggressive marketing make a heady combination. All too often we see people lured into buying things they don't really need or spending more than they can afford. They decide what they want without any regard to affordability. I came across one example of a holiday home in Spain that was up for re-sale. The reason? The purchasers paid a deposit and convinced themselves they could afford to proceed. They couldn't.

While there will always be those who get into debt problems, I am convinced there are many more who are in a "pre-debt problem" state of living for today and not building the inner confidence that comes from having some resources behind them. Yes we all want a bigger, better house, car, boat, plane and a helicopter on the back of the boat. There is no point being disappointed that we cannot have them. Leave the billionaires to their own problems.

There is absolutely nothing wrong with ambition and striving for success. But thinking one can live beyond one's means is not helpful at all. The impossible is impossible. (Unless you have the kind of money that says it isn't.)

Moderating one's ambitions to sensible steps means a greater chance of achieving both them and long term satisfaction: a) you are more likely to achieve each incremental step, b) your resolve is tested as you proceed and c) you are not over-stretched and d) you are less likely to make a huge decision that could turn out wrong.

Plan what you can afford
before deciding what you want

Forgive and forget, harbouring grudges only harms you

"Forgive and forget" must be one of the most well known quotations of all time. The small addition above is however noteworthy: harbouring grudges only harms you. In ocean yacht racing, where performance and indeed one's very survival are dependent on team work and collaboration, there is no room for arguments let alone grudges. Teams have different ways of dealing with this challenge - hence the phrase: "leave it on the next wave." This meant that at the first sign of an argument, anyone in the team was duty-bound to interject and tell people to leave their differences on the passing wave.

The problem with bearing grudges is that this mind-set changes one's personality. It harms people because they rarely see how it changes them. Slowly they become more stressed, less open and less happy people. The signals are evident and their friends start to distance themselves at the very time when more social contact would be so helpful.

Perhaps this is why it is so important to get over the inevitable setbacks that happen in life. My observation is that those who can bounce back lead much happier and more successful lives as a result. One example was an individual who was fired, said "Oh well, worse things can happen," then went on to set up his own business and retired a millionaire.

Life is too short to have distractions caused by retained bad memories. No one likes people who appear bitter and twisted. Get over it; move on.

Forgive and forget,
harbouring grudges
only harms you

There have been some terrible moments in my life, a few of which actually happened

This quotation begs the question: what is the source of terror? Reality is very often different to perception because terror is a construct of the mind. The terrible moments were inner moments, created in the mind. It is interesting to note that only a few of the allegedly terrible moments actually happened. It might be instructive to think about the ratio between imagined terror and actual terror. I have always suspected it to be hundreds to one. People can only terrorise you psychologically if you give them permission. If you deny permission then they are just shouting at themselves.

Again, human nature assumes worse than the worst. People with inner strength have a knack of stepping back, reflecting and an ability to see things in their wider context. Then they appear to see things in other contexts hitherto unseen by many other people altogether. It is this ability to step out of the immediate cause of terror that is so liberating, so calming, so strengthening. Rather than have their energies sapped they obtain renewal from this sense of perspective.

Perhaps one of the greatest values of perspective is the sense of relative intensity: while a situation may appear to terrorise at the time, the "terror" may be small compared with other events that could have happened. Even if the "terror" is substantial and what actually happened was serious, there are still wider contexts that could have been more extreme. By drawing on one's experience of other difficult situations, this undoubtedly informs one's assessment and plans for solving the immediate issue. As one draws together an action plan or a solution, slowly the "terror" reduces. Action conquers fear.

There have been some terrible
moments in my life,
a few of which
actually happened

I have served my apprenticeship in the school of angst.
I don't need that any more. I've graduated

There comes a time in most people's lives when they are at ease with their lot in life. No more the obsessive striving for money, status, power, "more" of everything. They realise that the pursuit of materialism comes with a cost. This is a human cost – hence the reference to angst.

The question is: when does one feel one has also served one's apprenticeship in the school of angst? The use of the words "apprenticeship" and "school" give a helpful indication: that all things have their time and place. They also give a hint of adult wisdom implying that such tendencies are the domain of school children, the playground, and childishness. If we accept that people don't change, only the date – it is easier to appreciate that in some cases behaviour in intense environments may be childishly predictable – and one may tire of this, preferring a different environment.

The notion of having graduated is also instructive. This suggests a "rite de passage" to something better, more mature and more adult. It also contains a mild rebuke as if to say "now then children, I am a post-graduate – I've been there, done it and got the T shirt!"

Inner strength means being able to step outside the immediate pressures and silly games people play. It does not mean ignoring responsibilities, tasks and actions. It does not mean shirking hard work. But it can mean that hard work is easier and less political where one can step aside from childish behaviour.

I have served my apprenticeship
in the school of angst.
I don't need that any more.
I've graduated

Sometimes the very thing you're looking for is the one thing you can't see

It pays to turn the periscope around. Sometimes a single-minded focus on a narrow goal can mean missing opportunities. I once overheard a conversation that went like this: "Are you married?" "I'm too busy at work to find that special person." "But maybe if you were married you wouldn't have to work so hard?" "I need to get on in my career" "What if your spouse could provide everything you need?" At that point, the penny dropped and the look on the person's face said "Oh my god what am I doing here?" It was as if their whole raison d'être had been holed below the water line.

By asking for feedback from trusted friends and colleagues, one can mitigate the risk of a rude awakening. That of course assumes one has trusted friends and colleagues. But people with inner strength do have them and they have the ability to laugh at themselves rather than leave that to others.

Having check points along the way is always a good idea. If navigation systems use them, then why not people? It was an early Roman philosopher who said "If a man does not know to which port he is steering, no wind is favourable to him."

It has also been said that the great is the enemy of the good. A perfectly satisfactory, even very good thing, person or relationship can be eclipsed by something even better. The comparative inferiority does not remove the good qualities from that which is good. And the pursuit of the ultimate may come with a superior cost. I am not advocating mediocrity. Simply the ability to recognise what is good when one sees it.

Sometimes the very thing
you're looking for
is the one thing you can't see

The commuters, you look in their eyes on a Friday. There's nothing there

Some metropolitan centres are so big; people think nothing of travelling for up to two hours to get to work. London, Sao Paulo and Tokyo spring to mind but there are many other cities where this is the case. Other cultures have this much less. I think city workers in Spain are among the most resistant to working far from their homes.

For those who travel on the London underground and then the suburban commuter trains, the daily monotony takes a toll. Some people are totally absorbed in their own ipod / ipad / iphone world, while others are talking – but on a cell phone not to anyone on the train. By the time Friday comes around, the trains are quieter and when I look into the eyes of the person opposite I frequently see nothing there. I have even had someone staring back at me without them realising they were actually asleep with their eyes open! I wonder how many weigh up the true cost of this.

The London Evening Standard (the evening paper) even published a series of articles on commuter romance. Readers would write messages addressed to "the guy on the 19:50 from Waterloo to Reading with......" this was because they did not have the courage to speak to the person directly. I find this amusing because my parents met for the very first time on a train. My father said to my mother "that's quite a strong pair of glasses you have." She replied, "Yes, the image forms in front of the retina." It is strange to think that my very existence stems from these two sentences.

The commuters, you
look in their eyes on a Friday.
There's nothing there

Quality is remembered long after the price is forgotten

Everyone likes a good deal; good value or a bargain. But as with most things, if you buy something that exactly matches your needs and it has the good design and overall quality to last, it is the quality that is remembered. I think the same can apply to intangible things: quality of interaction, quality of ideas, quality of personality and quality of life.

Whatever the "cost" of meeting someone, doing business with them, having fun with them – I think quality is what gets remembered. Think about when and where you were happiest: was it because of huge expense on a luxurious holiday or was it due to the quality of a moment shared with someone? Was it because of monetary expenditure or not having to be concerned about day-to-day matters?

People who think about their own personal branding – what they stand for and what they are remembered for, usually want to excel at something and be noted for it. They make sure certain qualities are understood and are visible, so as to underpin their own brand equity.

We will always meet others for whom getting the lowest possible cost is top priority. I think they sometimes need some education on the risks attached to this approach.

Perhaps having fewer things of higher quality also builds for a less stressful life. When you know you can rely on something or someone, you feel far more in control. Inner strength comes from knowing who and what you can rely upon.

> **Quality is remembered
> long after the price is forgotten**

Some people are so clever; they can't see how stupid they are

Some people are such narrow deep introverted specialists, they are virtually unemployable. But this quotation refers to a different characteristic. Some are so sure and dogmatic that they are incapable of seeing the bigger picture. They are prepared to be an intellectual bully just to prove their point. Sadly, in organisations, people get hired for their technical capability and fired for their interpersonal ineptitude.

"Wining the battle but losing the war" is instructive. The relentless pursuit of dogma destroys pragmatism. There was a Frenchman and an Englishman. They were playing boules in the rural French town square. The Englishman wanted planning permission to convert and restore an old barn. The Mayor had been very difficult and the Englishman had failed to appreciate the cultural, community and civic importance of the Mayor. So he decided to take his revenge on his French opponent. He knew his application was perfectly in order. He knew everything was administratively correct; he had paid good money to ensure it was perfect. He knew the Mayor was being obstructive for no objective reason.

Half way through the game, a trusted friend made one final attempt to counsel the Englishman. At last the penny dropped and despite high energy and emotion, he lost to his opponent. Cheers went up from the crowd of French onlookers as they all retired to the auberge. The Englishman bought drinks all round, to discover his opponent was a close friend of the Mayor. It was then finally that he understood that by losing, he had won. That was his entré into French rural life, which otherwise would have remained firmly closed.

Some people are so clever;
they can't see
how stupid they are

Adversity cleanses the lethargies of man

I have heard of countries, organisations and individuals being described as "fat, dumb and happy" ie: complacent. They suffer from "group think" – the tendency to deny controversy and squash open rigorous debate. They reject criticism and establish elaborate cultural mechanisms to marginalise those who go against the prevailing orthodoxy. And there lies the seed of destruction.

However once the burning platform for change is appreciated, such lethargies can be reduced if not swept away. People with inner strength recognise the need for change and for their own physical strength to engage with the immense challenge or test to come. In appreciating the scope of adversity, lethargy evaporates as they adopt leadership positions – either formally or informally. They realise that the time to deal with a problem is before it becomes a bigger one.

I have also observed strong individuals whose sense of resolve is renewed against the adversity of moral, ethical or professional wrong doing. They are prepared to make a stand but do so in a way that is constructive.

If you have ever been a part of a team or organisation that is on the brink of failure, you may understand the motivating power of adversity. Now more than ever, these tests are upon us. It is illuminating to learn how people cope with them. Some adopt leadership positions, others are secretly subversive, some overtly disruptive and others go into denial. People with inner strength usually "get it" – they understand what needs to be done but do not panic as they know there is no point fuelling anxiety. They focus on the job at hand.

Adversity cleanses
the lethargies of man

If you are going to live your life like a fighter pilot you may want to check your parachute first

In a literal sense, given the likelihood of being shot down, it would be sensible for our pilot to check all the safety equipment. Metaphorically, those who live everything in fast forward may also need to take stock of their own safety systems. You may well argue that to compete, we all now have to live like a fighter pilot. But everything is relative and I am interested in the extremes relative to normality, even if it is today's new definition of normality.

In the event of sudden, possibly catastrophic change, do people have an adequate support mechanism of family, relations, friends and contacts? Or – has their network dispersed through neglect? Most people recognise that high reward usually means high risk. Few fully appreciate what needs to be done to mitigate that risk. Further, if your behaviour has adapted to a ruthless cut-and-thrust "eat what you kill" culture, don't be surprised if the mercenary tendency is served back to you.

The inner strength characteristic is not to compromise one's ethics. It is to ensure that one's network, family, friends and even finances ie: the wider support mechanisms, are cultivated in proportion to the risk of getting shot down. By doing this, one can make more balanced decisions, behave with impartiality and without fear. All of which – interestingly – reduce the likelihood of having to use that parachute at all.

As a final thought, if you do have to use your parachute, what will you float down to? A "plan B" that is a calmer life? – or back to the runway? If you don't have a plan B, what does that tell you?

If you are going to live your life
like a fighter pilot
you may want to check your
parachute first

Life is no rehearsal. It's the main event

Carpe Diem! Or even seize the year, let alone the day or the moment. All too often one comes across people who have an "If only I had..." mentality. And as we know, it's the things we don't do that we regret. Too often, there is a tendency to hold back, to have self-doubt or some hesitation. Opportunities are lost and if attitudes are closed, one's mind–set can default to the negative.

Sometimes people need a push to get involved. When challenged with the "Can't" word, a typical response from people with inner strength is "What would you do if you were completely fearless and what is the first step along the way?" One approach is to step outside the immediate situation and look at it from the perspective of an observer. This meta mirror helps people to appreciate the transient nature of opportunity. It is hard to create or predict opportunity but preparation and openness mean one has more to go after when the co-incidence of opportunity meets preparation.

My observation is that people who understand this quotation are in the category of "happening to the world" rather than the world happening to them. The more people use their strength and courage the easier it gets. The principle of deferred gratification is fine early in life, through education and when establishing one's career but it is hardly surprising that organisations like SAGA (the organisation for the over 50s: holidays, financial services, networking and so on) have an advertising slogan "Now's the time." As with so many things explored in this book – it is a question of balancing priorities: everything in moderation, especially the moderation.

Life is no rehearsal.
It's the main event

Never rely on money to make you happy

Materialism is insatiable. The more you have, the more you need so it becomes a source of dissatisfaction rather than intrinsic satisfaction. My observation of people who are fulfilled is that they have deep meaningful relationships, are supported, have an extensive network and high self-esteem. Self-esteem transcends financial wealth and I have met some very wealthy but fundamentally unhappy people. A 2011 global survey found the happiest nation to be the Bangladeshis.

At my school, there were some boys (it was an independent boys school) whose wealthy parents gave them lavish presents. Whereas I had a contribution to a new bike for my 17th birthday, more than one of my colleagues had a brand new Triumph Spitfire two-seater sports car. Sadly, they seemed to do less well in later life and most got divorced before they were 40. Later in my career I met people whose relentless pursuit of riches led to questionable behaviour and a one-track personality. The lesson as ever appears to be: keep a sense of perspective and retain some balance — even if that is impossible in the short term.

If happiness is an abstract state of mind, it is folly to think it can be bought. There is more to it than that. I once had a holiday job as a painter's mate. While painting guttering on a Victorian house I was amazed at his wisdom, his satisfaction with life and his knowledge of his own capabilities. While he could not read or write, he was a master-craftsman, a genius and an artist with plaster. He showed me how to do work properly and how to spot cheating done by previous workmen. "Putty and paint can make the Devil a Saint" he warned. But he took immense pride in doing a good job.

Never rely on money to make you happy

There is no such thing as bad weather; only inappropriate clothing

Many people think this applies to the outdoors. At one level they are correct but don't be fooled. This quotation has deeper meaning for those of us interested in inner strength. If the bad weather is a metaphor for adversity and unexpected setbacks, then the clothing refers to the way in which we prepare and protect ourselves against them.

To continue the metaphor, ask yourself whether your protection against adversity is as thin as a T-shirt or the latest Gore-Tex storm-proof mountaineering jacket. Such protection will be known from previous quotations. But just as sometimes we go out with inappropriate clothing, sometimes we are ill prepared for sudden changes in other aspects of life. The inner strength way is of course to expect the unexpected and to be prepared.

Resilience comes from both preparation – being one step ahead and also from experience. Strong people are those who learn from experience and demonstrate the learning. Also, they have the flexibility of mind to work with the adverse conditions and use them to advantage: you can't stop snow but you can learn to ski. Today's economic and business climate is demanding. A resilient approach is required. Adopting the mentality of "no such thing as bad weather" can be a highly uplifting attitude. It means that whatever life throws at you, you are prepared to have a go and not buckle or give in. Maybe that is what the army assault course was all about? More new businesses are started in recessions than when times are good. Perhaps that test of resolve is what drives innovation.

There is no such thing
as bad weather; only
inappropriate clothing

Laugh. It is the fastest way to start, renew and maintain friendship

Studies have shown that smiling at someone actually changes their hormone balance. Laughter changes one's own endorphin balance and positively affects others around you. Laughter is also a great way of reducing stress. Further, it helps people to step back and look at a situation from a different perspective – all key things in our quest for inner strength. As we have seen before, those who cannot laugh at themselves, leave the job to others. But there is more than this – laughing at other things is all about retaining an overall sense of humour.

Laughter projects an attractive quality that most people want. It also shows that you are enjoying yourself. People like to be around others who are "fun" to be with. People with high self-esteem and strength are usually able to see the humorous side of things more easily and show their emotions more readily. They don't have concerns about how they may be regarded.

Psychologists tell us that 7% of communication is verbal. The remaining 93% is non-verbal through facial expression, gesture, "body-language" and other aspects such as clothes. Laughter is a great means of communication that transcends words, culture and language. I have seen it work wonders in c50 countries.

So whenever you are in a stressful situation, find something to laugh about. It does not have to be directly about the situation, although that helps. Laughter reduces tension, builds strength, aids calmness and helps objectivity. It also enables people to see things from new perspectives that can lead to better solutions.

Laugh. It is the fastest way
to start, renew and
maintain friendship

Chance favours the prepared mind

We all experience fortuitous opportunity; what happens next is largely up to the individual. Whether an opportunity is grasped or rejected is a reflection of attitude, willingness, motivation and so on. The prepared mind is the most open but many people have surprisingly closed minds. Use of the question "why not?" is disappointingly rare. All too often people are reluctant to seize the initiative because "they" (ie: someone else) won't let them. And yet all power is taken not given, so walking into a hotel as if you own it is frequently a prelude to superior customer service. I am not advocating arrogance but the confidence to banish threshold fear.

A note from history says "They can because they think they can." An envoy was sent from the east cost of Mallorca to Ciutadella, the ancient west cost capital of Menorca. At nightfall, the envoy asked the city leaders to look to the horizon to see his army's camp fires along the distant cost across the sea. Believing an immense army about to invade, they capitulated and signed a treaty. Little did they know the bonfires were just fires – there was no army.

Where people's mind-set is prepared for opportunity, they are more likely to embrace it successfully. Life can be very serendipitous – think about the circumstances of when you first met your future wife or husband. Seeing then seizing opportunity is very much a part of life being no rehearsal. It is also about recognising situations for what they are and what they could develop into. For example, does the book of inner strength remain just an idea, a scrappy collection of quotations, a proper list or the manuscript of a real book? Does it get published or stay a manuscript?

Chance favours
the prepared mind

Would you marry to please others or yourself?

This quotation comes from the early eighteenth century. The Spectator magazine had an agony aunt column. A reader submitted a very long question covering several pages. It explained how he had fallen for a very attractive young lady but because she had no fortune, he was in a dilemma regarding whether and how he could pursue her for marriage. He covered every social and cultural nuance of his agony, asking for advice on what to do as she was of lower status. The agony aunt replied with one line: the quotation above.

It is instructive beyond the story because it is a challenge to anyone thinking of nailing their colours to the mast on any particular topic. Before you overtly support something, someone, an ideology – ask yourself why you are doing it. Is it for your own strongly held reasons or for externally convenient reasons? The inner strength way is to adopt strong allegiance for one's own reasons – no one else's. Yet it is surprising how many ideological marriages of convenience there are.

An independent mind, an external as well as internal view and a strong personal value-set make this an easy topic for those with inner strength.

The quotation is also a warning not to make rash decisions that one might regret. After all – marry in haste, repent at leisure.

Would you marry
to please others
or yourself?

When there's a war on, it's performance that counts, nothing else

By way of balance, this last quotation is a recognition that despite our best efforts to lead controlled, calm, organised lives, with fun and well managed change – sometimes one has to go into extreme stretch. This is understandable and even acceptable for the right reasons. After all, life is a bed or roses – thorns and all. But when there is a "war" on, or you meet someone for whom there is a war, recognise that there are times when only performance counts.

Picture the scene: the Sea of Japan 1945, storm force 10, the battleship pitching and yawing in mountainous, thunderous waves. The Magazine is full of very unstable high explosive that relies on refrigeration to stabilise it and prevent it blowing up the whole ship. Then the refrigeration fails. The task for the Royal Navy? – fix the refrigeration in 10 hours or the ship goes down with no survivors. This is a real life example. Thankfully the "perform or die" instruction was carried out, and they lived. Sometimes it is important to recognise when a situation warrants all-out effort. There are times when it is necessary and it is also important to know when to stop. My collection of quotations is not arguing for the easy or lazy life, it is merely about making the most of what life is all about. And at times we all know it is very very difficult.

Remember also that you may encounter seemingly strange behaviour from people for whom there is a "war" and they are totally focused on winning it. For them, nothing else matters even though they may have a totally different perspective to your own.

When there's a war on, it's performance that counts, nothing else

Afterthoughts

I hope that by now you have formed a good view of the linkages between most, if not all of the quotations and aphorisms in this book. I firmly believe they are systemically linked. These connections have been made more overt in the later explanations and illustrations for each example. I hope the themes act as a key to unlock so much that is hidden when one takes things only at face value. This includes things that are hidden from others and hidden from ourselves. By being able to stand back and appreciate context, so much more becomes apparent and this contributes to deeper understanding.

People I admire for their inner strength have a rare mix of the following: first and foremost, high self-esteem, then the ability to step back from the immediate. They are interested in context as an explanation for the behaviour of others. They are able to say "no" with calm confidence as well as "yes." They have a strong sense of personal values and ethics. They are focused and not distracted. They also understand the principles of diminishing returns, knowing when to stop and how to learn from mistakes. When they have to fight, they make sure they can win and when there is a war on, they know that only performance counts. They try to achieve things without creating unnecessary work and they have a stable home life with strong relationships and support from both family and an extensive network. They understand that change is a constant and so they are open to it. As a result, their inner strength is visible because they are not de-railed by the trials of life. They get over the inevitable set backs and they learn from them. They are generous with their coaching and mentoring of others and above all are respected.

Finally they are not fashion victims who are easily led. They have a point of view and know what they want; as a result – they happen to the world rather than get blown around, pushed around making no impact.

Does this make them boringly predictable? I don't think so. I admire their relaxed calm confidence in a world of change and speed. Above all they retain a certain irreverence and a sense of humour. They don't take themselves too seriously. They still have time for fun.

Afterthoughts to the second edition

People tell me that this book's relevance increases and matures with time. Some have used it to carry immense adversity and hardship, including redundancy and bereavement. Others have learned to enjoy life anew, increasing their resolve and work rate. The world is a more difficult place in the mid 2010s than it was in 2007. Perhaps the value of simpler things and relationships has never been more important. And I don't mean to the exclusion of hard endeavour. By all means work that 80 hour week and the occasional "all-nighter" – but do rebalance and pay back the debt to your relationship bank accounts. I hope that in the new austerity, this work strikes a stronger chord. Or as someone said to me when Lehman Brothers collapsed: "How did you know we were heading this way when you wrote that book of inner strength?" I thought we were in a bubble and that things could not continue as they were. The more I look back at this work, the more grateful I am to the people who have helped by explaining their approach to life whether in Chile, Argentina, Brazil, Panama, the Caribbean, America, Europe, Russia, the Middle East, India, Singapore, Australia, China or Japan.

Maó, September 2012

Index: The quotations listed:

The quotations grouped.
Note: some appear more than once

Adversity
26, 32, 38, 54, 58, 70, 72, 76, 92, 108, 114, 126, 134, 142, 148,
232, 268, 282, 290, 300, 308

Conflict
82, 124, 160, 234, 238, 288, 312, 316

Eliminating Anxiety
14, 18, 42, 44, 48, 58, 70, 72, 74, 82, 92, 108, 116, 122, 134,
136, 142, 188, 194, 198, 208, 266, 268, 282, 288, 290, 304, 310

International
16, 34, 106, 128, 154, 166, 172, 176, 222, 254, 260, 274

Life balance
14, 18, 22, 48, 50, 84, 102, 120, 130, 152, 184, 202, 206, 208,
224, 236, 248, 252, 258, 264, 270, 280, 292, 304

Money
40, 48, 64, 86, 110, 118, 136, 162, 180, 212, 216, 218, 220, 226,
230, 284, 296, 306

New horizons
14, 18, 26, 32, 44, 54, 60, 72, 76, 88, 98, 108, 134, 142, 150,
170, 178, 200, 214, 228, 232, 256, 262, 268, 286, 304, 310, 312

Professional life

12, 14, 26, 36, 38, 42, 44, 54, 56, 58, 60, 62, 68, 72, 78, 80, 84, 88, 94, 96, 100, 104, 140, 142, 146, 164, 168, 170, 174, 176, 182, 188, 190, 192, 196, 200, 228, 244, 246, 250, 266, 272, 294

Relationships

20, 24, 28, 30, 52, 74, 90, 94, 116, 132, 144, 156, 158, 178, 188, 190, 194, 198, 210, 240, 278, 298, 310

Ian Muir is a senior business adviser. He works with top teams and individuals to improve organisational performance. He has worked across five continents having been an executive committee member at Charter International plc, a director of Cable & Wireless International Group Ltd, and a Trustee of a £2.2bn pension fund. He is a graduate of Bath University, a fellow of the Chartered Institute of Personnel and Development and a member of the European Mentoring and Coaching Council. Ian is the Founder Director at Keeldeep Associates Limited www.keeldeep.com a specialist advisory firm on top team development with the purpose of "surfacing effectiveness." He is an alumnus of INSEAD and a visiting fellow at London Metropolitan University Business School. Outside business, his interests include music, oil painting, photography, cooking, skiing and boating. Among his achievements he cites skiing Argentière from Croix de L'ognan (1972m) to Les Grands Montets base station (1236m) faster than the cable car, hanging one of his paintings in a City boardroom and coaching his wife from refusing to go on a cross-channel ferry to skippering a 40 tonne powerboat out of sight of land in just 5 years.